Contents

W9-DCJ-634

Welcome to Hampton Court Palace

...where you get two palaces for the price of one. The rose red brick Tudor palace is indelibly associated with Henry VIII. The baroque palace, first occupied in 1700, has some of the world's greatest gardens around it. This is a palace filled with stories and delights.

What to see

To help you make the most of your day at Hampton Court Palace we've devised some special tours of the most important spaces and places, so you don't miss anything!

See this amazing painted ceiling over the Queen's Staircase.

Tour 1:
Henry VIII at Hampton Court Palace

Walk in the footsteps of England's most famous king. Join the wedding celebrations for his sixth marriage to Kateryn Parr. Explore the story of the handsome prince in Young Henry VIII's Story and discover Henry's magnificent state apartments of the 1530s.
Pages 14-21

Tour 2:
Henry VIII's Kitchens

This massive 'food factory' produced over 1,200 meals a day for a hungry royal court. Follow the production line and understand how raw food came in at one end of the kitchens and was sent out at the other, transformed into wonderful dishes fit for a royal court.
Pages 30-3

Tour 3:
William III's Apartments

Follow the courtier's route: seeking an audience with the King, you climb the magnificent stairs into the impressively decorated guard room, passing through chambers ever more richly furnished, until you reach the intimate rooms where the King would drink and relax with his closest friends.
Pages 38-43

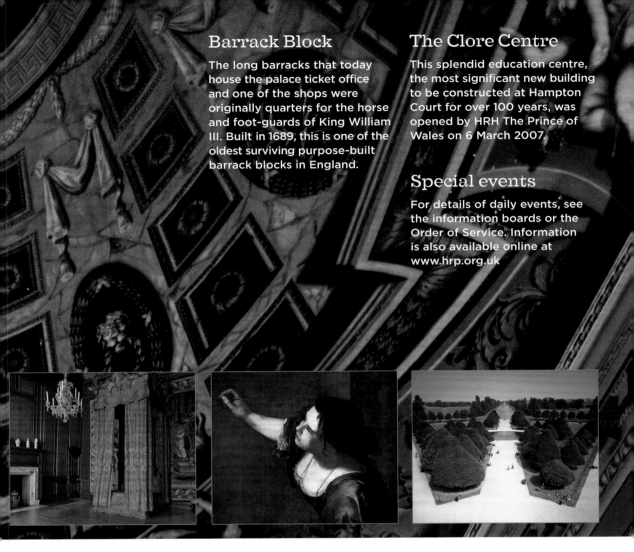

Barrack Block

The long barracks that today house the palace ticket office and one of the shops were originally quarters for the horse and foot-guards of King William III. Built in 1689, this is one of the oldest surviving purpose-built barrack blocks in England.

The Clore Centre

This splendid education centre, the most significant new building to be constructed at Hampton Court for over 100 years, was opened by HRH The Prince of Wales on 6 March 2007.

Special events

For details of daily events, see the information boards or the Order of Service. Information is also available online at www.hrp.org.uk

Tour 4:
The Georgian Story

Explore the public and private world of the Georgians, where court intrigues, political battles and bitter family rivalries were played out in some of the grandest rooms in the palace.
Pages 44-49

Tour 5:
Paintings at the palace

There has always been great art at Hampton Court, and the palace remains the home to some astonishing paintings from the 16th to the early 18th centuries. This short introductory tour will help you discover some of our 'must-see' highlights.
Pages 54-59

Tour 6:
The Gardens and Maze

Begin an enjoyable stroll around the beautiful palace gardens at the East Front, as you step out into one of the most instantly recognisable gardens in England. From the exquisitely planted Pond Garden to the gnarled branches of the ancient Great Vine, the 24 hectares of grounds will astound and delight you. Don't forget to leave enough time to escape the fiendish Maze!
Pages 62-5

A short history of
Hampton Court Palace

Over seven centuries the powerful owners of Hampton Court have changed the palace according to their demands or tastes. Yet curiously for a palace no one managed to wipe out entirely their predecessors' marks. They valued it for its rural setting and the prospect of hunting, and tolerated, even revered its hotchpotch of building styles. This gives the palace its unique romantic appeal, with reminders of its turbulent past at every turn.

Henry VIII's Great Hall

Medieval Hampton Court:
From crusader knights to Cardinal's palace

Buried beneath the palace are remains of the first known house, built for the Knights Hospitallers of St John sometime before 1338. This was the centre of a large farm estate owned by this holy order's priory, which was originally created to provide funds for crusaders in the Holy Land. In 1494 Giles Daubeney, one of King Henry VII's most senior courtiers, leased Hampton Court and it is from his time that we see the earliest parts of the palace.

Thomas Wolsey acquired Hampton Court in 1514. He was the most dominant churchman and politician in the land having risen quickly from fairly humble origins. He gained enormous power and wealth as Henry VIII's indispensable administrator and as a cardinal. He quickly began to turn the manor house into a palace in which to entertain his King and receive foreign dignitaries.

To accommodate the King, as well as his own household, Wolsey added a great new entrance courtyard. He built the first long gallery overlooking new gardens and hung the palace with several hundred fine tapestries, taking advantage of a diplomatic mission to France. These were changed every week, according to one impressed observer.

By 1525 Hampton Court was truly a palace and Wolsey formally presented it to the King, though Wolsey continued to add to the building. Being a cardinal he also created a new chapel with a cloister for state processions. All this was ready for an important ambassadorial visit by the French in 1527, part of negotiations towards a permanent peace treaty which Henry needed to support his attempts to divorce Queen Katherine of Aragon. This was the start of the end for Wolsey. He was unable to persuade the Pope to annul the royal marriage and in 1529 Henry removed him from Hampton Court once and for all.

Left: William III's newly completed baroque palace and gardens, from a view by Leonard Knyff, c1702.

Above: These painted stone arms outside the chapel belonged to Jane Seymour, Henry VIII's third wife.

Left: Henry dining in state in his Presence Chamber, surrounded by courtiers – as recalled by his court painter, Hans Holbein.

Below: The baptism procession for the baby Prince Edward which took place at Hampton Court in 1537. His half-sister Mary, later Queen of England, follows the canopy.

Henry VIII at Hampton Court:
A palace fit for a king

Henry VIII (reigned 1509-47) now began to take much more personal interest in his palace, which he was already preparing for his mistress and intended queen, Anne Boleyn. In the next decade greater sums than ever were spent – the equivalent of many millions of pounds today – to create a suitably magnificent setting. New queen's lodgings were planned, a chamber for the King's Council – the centre of government – and vastly enlarged kitchens to serve the new Great Hall. The King also desired greater privacy and created privy (private) lodgings for himself, complete with hot and cold running water, a rare thing at the time.

As a young man Henry had been keen on sports, but in his forties he was less eager to risk himself at tournaments. At this time he built himself a new indoor real (royal) tennis court and two bowling alleys.

Queen Anne was never to use her new apartments for she fell from grace and was executed for treason in 1536, following trumped-up charges that included adultery committed at Hampton Court. At last in 1537 the new queen, Jane Seymour, provided a male heir, Prince Edward, who was baptised in the Chapel Royal, beneath its celestial new ceiling.

After Jane's untimely death following childbirth, Henry's great building project soon came to a close. Later it was here that he divorced Anne of Cleves after another all-too brief marriage in 1540, and it was at Hampton Court too that Catherine Howard's infidelity was reported to the King in his chamber by the Archbishop of Canterbury. Finally, in 1543, the marriage of Henry and Kateryn Parr took place at the palace. Four years later the old king was dead and a young boy sat on the throne.

Prince Edward, later King Edward VI, at the age of one by Hans Holbein.

Charles I's (reigned 1625-49) greatest contribution to the palace was his art collecting, especially works by Italian masters. He was the first English king to do this, astutely buying Mantegna's renowned *Triumphs of Caesar*.

After the Civil War and Charles's execution, most of the valuable royal goods were sold for the benefit of the Commonwealth. Curiously the leader of the Parliamentary army, Oliver Cromwell, kept back the palace and some of its greatest treasures for his own pleasure and lived here like a king.

With the Restoration in 1660 the pleasure-loving Charles II (reigned 1660-85) added a new tennis court to the attractions of his greatest palace and hunting park. A year later Anne Boleyn's old apartments were prepared for Charles's honeymoon with his Portuguese queen, Catherine of Braganza.

The 16th and 17th-century palace:
From boy prince to republic and Restoration

Edward VI (reigned 1547-53) was only 9 when he came to the throne and was put under the care and direction of his uncle, the Duke of Somerset, who was appointed Lord Protector. Somerset took over the Queen's Apartments at Hampton Court when the court stayed at the palace during the summer.

It was at Hampton Court Palace that Edward's Catholic half-sister Queen Mary I (reigned 1553-8) accepted King Philip II of Spain's offer of marriage and here that she was confined during her 'phantom' pregnancy in 1555. No baby arrived; she was in fact fatally ill and died three years later.

Mary's half-sister, Elizabeth I (reigned 1558-1603) had been forced to stay at Hampton Court during Mary's false pregnancy, following suspicions of involvement in a rebellion. She held little affection for the palace, but this pragmatic queen did make her mark with some improvements to her father's great palace – a new privy kitchen and a coach house, for the latest mode of transport.

King James I (reigned 1603-25) spent his first Christmas as king at Hampton Court, where he and the court were entertained by plays and masques given by his private theatre company, the 'King's Men', which included William Shakespeare. In January 1604 the King attended to more serious business at the Hampton Court Conference, a somewhat staged religious debate that resulted in the King James translation of the Bible.

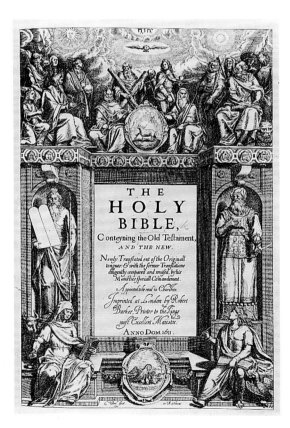

The King James or Authorised Version of the Bible was the most far-reaching legacy of the Hampton Court Conference of 1604.

Queen Anne shown as Justice, from the Queen's Drawing Room, painted by Antonio Verrio around 1705.

Baroque palace:
The last Stuarts and the Hanoverians

James II (reigned 1685-8), Charles II's brother, used Hampton Court little, but it was his foolhardy actions – in particular his self-professed Roman Catholicism – that led to the most enormous change at the palace. In 1688 James was ousted to France in the Glorious Revolution. His daughter, Mary II (jointly reigned 1689-d1694), and her Dutch husband, William of Orange (William III, reigned 1689-1702) were eager to see their ancient palace and immediately set about rebuilding it on a grand scale. They turned to the architect Sir Christopher Wren, whose office designed an ambitious new palace inspired by the baroque palaces of rival Louis XIV of France. In the end the cost led to only half the palace being rebuilt.

For the first part of the reign Mary oversaw much of the work, while William fought abroad. After five years Mary died suddenly of smallpox, aged only 32, leaving the King distraught and the palace unfinished. William completed his rooms six years later but used them for just two years before he too died suddenly after a fall from his horse in the park.

When Queen Anne (reigned 1702-14) succeeded to the throne she did not much like her brother-in-law's palace, nor the huge bills left unpaid. Nevertheless she did complete some of his works, including part of the queen's side where her husband, Prince George of Denmark, could entertain. Anne herself rarely stayed at Hampton Court until in her last years, when this pious queen completed the modernisation of the chapel.

The new king, George I (reigned 1714-27) was also unenthusiastic about Hampton Court. He brought no queen and disliked the very public life he was expected to lead. Instead his son, the Prince of Wales and his princess finally completed the Queen's Apartments for their rival court. The King responded by turning the Great Hall into a permanent theatre.

Though George II (reigned 1727-60) and Queen Caroline filled the palace with their family and favourites, Hampton Court was already in terminal decline. They left their mark with the Tudor revival-style lodgings for their favourite son, the Duke of Cumberland, but after the highly-cultivated Caroline's death in 1737, King George rarely stayed. His grandson, George III, reputedly had bad memories of his childhood at Hampton Court and never liked the palace. Instead he formalised the system of granting unused apartments to courtiers who were deserving of royal 'grace and favour'. (See page 66)

19th to 21st centuries:
A people's palace

No British monarch ever lived here again and for two centuries Hampton Court became an unlikely village of well-to-do ladies (mostly widows) with royal connections. (Charles Dickens called them 'gypsies of gentility' in *Little Dorrit*.) In 1839, Queen Victoria opened the palace to large numbers of paying visitors, though it had always been accessible to the well-to-do. Over the Victorian era Hampton Court was gradually restored as people came to value its place in history.

At the end of the 20th century the preservation of these ancient buildings seemed assured. However, the palace administration was put to the test with a terrible fire in 1986 that severely damaged the King's Apartments. Expert salvage and conservation work, taking several years, ensured that the palace emerged as beautiful as before, and with a greater understanding of its past.

Above: On Easter Day 1986 fire broke out in a grace-and-favour residence above the King's Apartments. Much of the roof collapsed, badly damaging the state rooms and their furnishings. Sadly the occupant, Lady Gale, perished in the blaze.

Left: Often characterised as genteel older ladies, the family of grace-and-favour residents often spanned generations. This is probably Lady Keyes – photographed by her daughter Madeline in 1906.

Katherine of Aragon – Henry's first wife, discarded after 20 years of marriage because she could not give him a son.

Anne Boleyn – the lady who loved to say no, but even Henry's most scheming wife could not escape execution in 1536.

Jane Seymour – betrothed to Henry at Hampton Court, and she died there a little over a year later after giving him a longed-for son.

Anne of Cleves – rather too homely for Henry's taste. The couple separated almost immediately.

Catherine Howard – Ageing Henry fell deeply in love, but his pride was bitterly hurt by this flirty teenager, who paid a terrible price for her alleged adultery.

Kateryn Parr – the king's last wife, who outlived her husband.

Meet Henry VIII

Leading historian Dr David Starkey introduces the king who made the most headlines in history – and the six women he loved and lost.

It makes one of the world's great stories. Prince Charming turns into Bluebeard. More far-fetched than the plotline in any soap opera, it has the sex and violence of X-rated cinema. It is a great love story and a political thriller where hearts, lives, wealth and power are all at stake. The characters come straight from central casting: the playboy, the monster, the saint, the schemer, the doormat, the dim fat one, the sexy teen and the swot. It is the story of King Henry VIII and his six wives, and much of the drama was played out at Hampton Court.

It is not just a bodice-ripping yarn. The reign of Henry VIII was as big a turning point in English history as was the Norman Conquest. England became a Protestant nation. The pious Catholic King who had been spiritual subject to the Pope in Rome turned himself into the political and religious leader of his own people. And all because the lady loved to say no until the ring was nearly on her finger.

Wife number one, Katherine of Aragon was Henry's consort for over two decades, but she could not give him the son and dynastic security he craved and was discarded. Her presence is in the exhibition in the rooms once occupied by Cardinal Wolsey, whose palace this had been, and in the top floor rooms designed for her overlooking Clock Court. The break with Rome came in the process of ridding the King of her. Anne Boleyn's initials intertwined with Henry's in a lover's knot

decorate the arch that bears her name. Hardly was her corpse cold, executed on trumped-up charges of adultery and incest and also for only providing a daughter, before Jane Seymour took her place. Jane left a son, born at Hampton Court, but she died there, too ill to witness Prince Edward's grand baptism procession. The search was on for another queen: Europe was scoured, Anne of Cleves was found – and was found sadly wanting. She continued to live post-divorce at court, after the marriage of the teenage Catherine Howard to the now bloated king. Anne was soon to know that Catherine had been arrested at the palace for adultery and taken away for execution but she probably never saw the unhappy ghost that is said to run screaming to the door of the Chapel Royal. Finally, Kateryn Parr, the true Protestant among the wives, occupied the rooms that Wolsey had once had. Only Anne of Cleves and Kateryn Parr outlived their husband.

Tour 1:
Henry VIII
at Hampton Court Palace

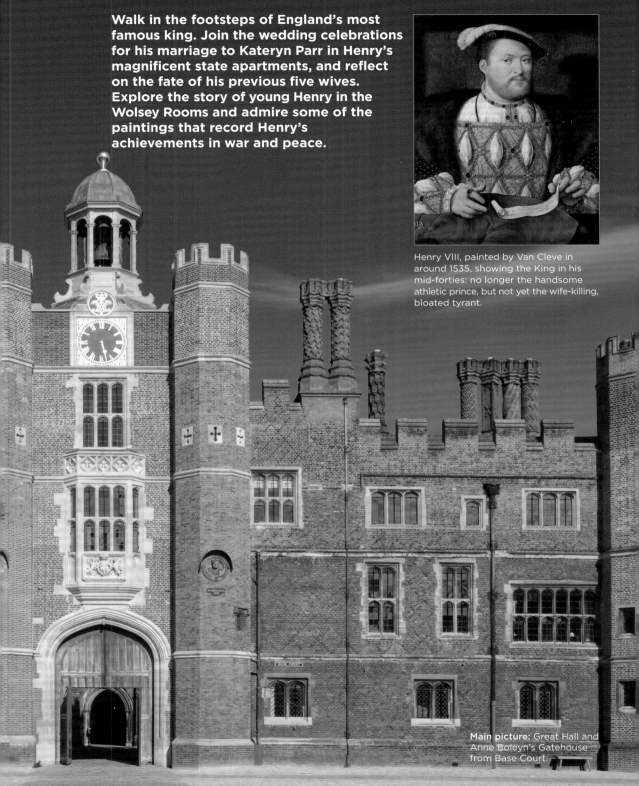

Walk in the footsteps of England's most famous king. Join the wedding celebrations for his marriage to Kateryn Parr in Henry's magnificent state apartments, and reflect on the fate of his previous five wives. Explore the story of young Henry in the Wolsey Rooms and admire some of the paintings that record Henry's achievements in war and peace.

Henry VIII, painted by Van Cleve in around 1535, showing the King in his mid-forties: no longer the handsome athletic prince, but not yet the wife-killing, bloated tyrant.

Main picture: Great Hall and Anne Boleyn's Gatehouse from Base Court.

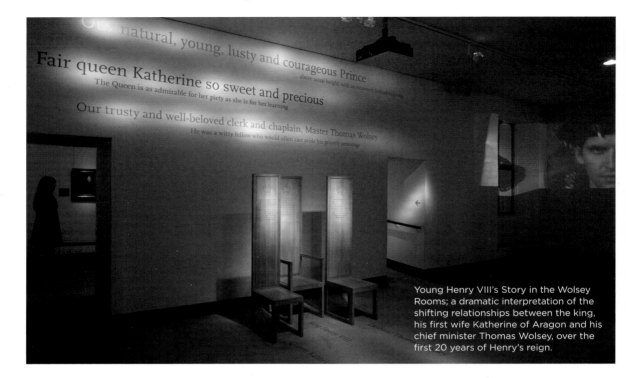

natural, young, lusty and courageous Prince
above usual height, with an extremely fine calf to his leg

Fair queen Katherine so sweet and precious
The Queen is as admirable for her piety as she is for her learning

Our trusty and well-beloved clerk and chaplain, Master Thomas Wolsey
He was a witty fellow who would often cast aside his priestly personage

Young Henry VIII's Story in the Wolsey Rooms; a dramatic interpretation of the shifting relationships between the king, his first wife Katherine of Aragon and his chief minister Thomas Wolsey, over the first 20 years of Henry's reign.

For many people, Hampton Court Palace *is* Henry VIII. It is indeed the great brick façade of Henry's Tudor palace that looms in front of the visitor today from the west. Inside, Henry VIII's private rooms may have been swept away by the 'improvements' commissioned by later monarchs, but Henry VIII's great hall, chapel and watching chamber still survive, as well as an earlier suite of apartments built by Thomas Wolsey.

The Wolsey Rooms
Young Henry VIII

Before the emergence of the Henry VIII of popular history – the fat raging brute of a tyrant who married six times – there was another Henry. 'Young' Henry VIII was athletic, charismatic and handsome. For the first 20 years of his reign he was married to Katherine of Aragon and guided by his close friend Thomas Wolsey.

The story of Young Henry VIII is told at Hampton Court through the eyes and experiences of its three lead characters in the Wolsey Rooms, part of the 'original' Hampton Court Palace, built by Thomas Wolsey in the 1520s for his own use.

The rooms

Wolsey was a brilliant administrator with one eye for detail and another for opportunity: the most powerful minister in England, a cardinal and papal legate. He started building Hampton Court in 1514, and it was probably in these rooms that Wolsey negotiated state business.

The Wolsey Rooms are a mixture of formal reception rooms, with painted and gilded ceilings, and smaller more private spaces. The apartment once covered three floors and ended in a two-storey long gallery where the cardinal could walk and enjoy views of the gardens. Like the rest of the Tudor palace, these rooms were once lavishly decorated.

After Wolsey's fall from power, the Wolsey Rooms were enlarged and redecorated to provide lodgings for Princess Mary (later Mary I). They may also have been used by Henry's last queen, Kateryn Parr. They remained in residential use until the 1920s and were only afterwards restored to a more 'Tudor' character.

Tudor paintings at Hampton Court

In the Wolsey Rooms and Tudor state apartments you can find some of the most important history paintings to have survived from the reign of Henry VIII.

The Meeting of Henry VIII and the Emperor Maximilian I and *The Battle of the Spurs* record Henry VIII's victory over the French army of Louis XII in 1513. Seven years later, Henry was back in Europe, waging an even more vicious campaign of competitive hospitality at a peace summit with the new French king, Francis I. *The Embarkation of Henry VIII at Dover* and *The Field of Cloth of Gold* record Henry's attempts to show that he was the most magnificent prince in Europe.

The 'history' paintings are displayed with a selection of Tudor royal portraiture from the Royal Collection, including portraits of Henry VII, Henry VIII, Katherine of Aragon, Anne Boleyn and Edward VI.

Above: *The Field of Cloth of Gold* of 1520 was probably the most ambitious, over-the-top European summit ever held. Twelve thousand members of the English and French court partied for three weeks. Little real diplomatic progress was made.

Left: *The Meeting of Henry VIII and the Emperor Maximilian I.* Henry and Maximilian appear twice in this painted record glorifying their joint exploits of 1513: meeting each other astride their resplendent horses in front of their assembled cavalry and infantry divisions. Paintings like this decorated public royal apartments, reminding visiting diplomats of Henry's military might.

Look out for the 'Eavesdroppers' – the carved and painted heads that decorate the Great Hall roof.

Horn Room
This room was originally built as a waiting place for servants bringing food to the Great Hall. The staircase from the kitchens still has its original oak steps. The horns now on display here date back to the 17th century.

Above: The Great Hall owes much of its appearance today to a restoration undertaken in the 1840s.

Henry VIII's Apartments
The Great Hall

In the 16th century, Hampton Court was a palace, a hotel, a theatre and a vast entertainment complex. The Great Hall was, by itself, all of these things. It was used, every day, as the staff canteen for the lower ranks of Henry's court. Up to 600 people ate here in two sittings, twice a day. On special occasions, however, the tapestries were rolled out over the walls, candelabra were strung across the ceiling on wires, and the lights from hundreds of candles transformed the hall into a magical setting for a fantastical court masque.

The Great Hall is the largest room in the palace, 32m (106ft) long, 12m (40ft) wide and over 18m (60ft) high. A vast team of masons, carpenters, bricklayers and labourers began to build it for Henry VIII in the 1530s. The hammer-beam roof, designed by the King's Master Carpenter James Nedeham, was painted blue, red and gold.

The Abraham tapestries which line the walls today were commissioned by Henry himself, and probably first hung here for the visit of a large French embassy in 1546. This was just one of the magnificent state occasions when all the great rooms of Hampton Court were filled with the 'swaggering theatre' of court life. The Great Hall played host to dance and drama, with Henry himself earlier in his reign playing a starring role in specially written chivalric inventions, rescuing helpless maidens from dangerous castles.

James I at Hampton Court

Court entertainment did not die with Henry VIII. The Stuart court also used Henry VIII's Great Hall for some of the most important, expensive and elaborate theatricals ever staged at an English royal court. Shakespeare appeared here more than once before James I, as one of the King's Men, while Inigo Jones and Ben Jonson designed extravagant, and infamous, court masques. Dancing and drinking until dawn, the Stuart court was later described (from the Puritanical safety of the Commonwealth era) as a 'nursery of lust and intemperance'!

When the Stuart court had finished dancing, the partygoers piled into the Great Watching Chamber to eat. One observer records them pouncing on the food 'like so many harpies ... they upset the table and the crash of glass platters reminded me precisely of a severe hailstorm at Midsummer smashing the window glass'.

Great Watching Chamber
The artist Joseph Nash reconstructed this scene of Cardinal Wolsey and his household dining from his imagination (although the ceiling is instantly recognisable). The painting was published in 1839 in *The Mansions of England in the Olden Time*.

Great Watching Chamber

The Great Watching Chamber got its name from its position as the first of the King's state apartments beyond the Great Hall, where members of the Yeomen of the Guard were stationed to 'watch' and control access. The doors at the end of the room once led to a sequence of chambers where Henry himself entertained guests, dined, read and slept.

William III's rebuilding of Hampton Court demolished Henry's more private apartments, and made considerable changes to the Great Watching Chamber too. The panelling, stained glass and fireplace are later additions, but the restored ceiling has survived and the tapestries that line the rooms are all from Thomas Wolsey's collection.

The processional route, Haunted Gallery and Council Chamber

The King's 'Coming Forth' from his apartments to the chapel, on Sundays and special holy days, became the principal occasion when Henry VIII made himself visible to his wider court. Courtiers would lie in wait along the route to be seen by the King.

In 1541, Catherine Howard, Henry's fifth wife, discovered that she was to be charged with adultery. Legend has it that the young queen ran along the processional route in the hope of finding Henry in the chapel, to plead her innocence. Just before she reached the door she was seized by guards who took her screaming back to her rooms. Her ghost still, allegedly, haunts the gallery.

A small room to one side was used by the royal pages, whose duties included waiting on the courtiers in the Great Watching Chamber next door. This room is displayed as it might have looked in the 1540s. A larger room further down the gallery was Henry's Council Chamber, where some of the pivotal political decisions of his reign were made.

This re-creation of Henry VIII's Crown of State is on display in the Royal Pew. The original crown was worn by the King at Hampton Court for court ceremonies, including the feast of Epiphany on 6 January, when he would process to the Chapel Royal in full regalia.

The Chapel Royal

Hampton Court's royal chapel remains in active use today. In fact, it has been in continuous use ever since Thomas Wolsey built it almost 500 years ago. Henry VIII installed the magnificent vaulted ceiling here in the 1530s, and Queen Anne refurnished the interior of the chapel in the early 1700s.

The royal family did not sit in the main body of the church. A royal pew was provided on first-floor level, as part of the state apartments. In Tudor times, there was one large room for the king and one for the queen. Today, a single central room, like a box at an opera, is reserved for the monarch, with rooms on either side for gentlemen and ladies of the court. The ceiling of the central room was painted by Sir James Thornhill for Queen Anne with a playful scene of cherubs holding aloft a crown and a sword.

The east end of the chapel once contained a great double window filled with stained glass, with images of Henry VIII, Katherine of Aragon and Thomas Wolsey. The glass was destroyed in the Commonwealth and the window eventually bricked up. It is now completely hidden by the large oak reredos carved by Grinling Gibbons for Queen Anne.

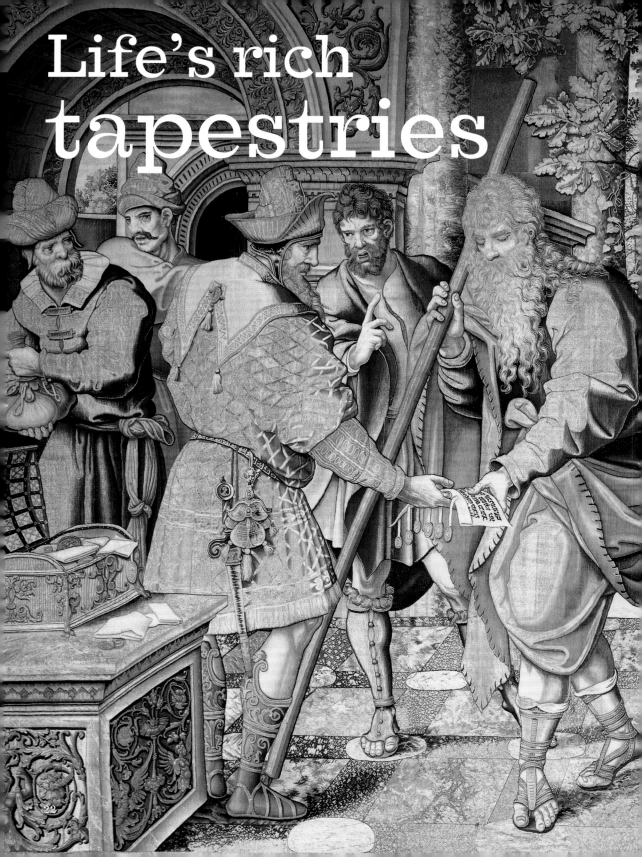

Life's rich tapestries

Left: Detail from *The Purchase of the Fields of Ephron* in the story of Abraham. Henry VIII commissioned one of the greatest sets of Brussels tapestries around 1540. He identified his own situation with the biblical patriarch.

Right: *The Triumph of Hercules*. The King would have enjoyed both the ultra-modern, Italian designs for the *Triumphs of the Gods* and comparison with the athletic hero, Hercules.

Hangynge aboute the walles Clothes of golde and palles, Arras of ryche aray, Fresshe as flours in May;

From *Colin Clout* by John Skelton, 1521-2
[palles – cloth covering; arras – fine tapestry]

King Henry VIII amassed an immense collection of tapestries; at Hampton Court you will find the precious survivors. As curator Sebastian Edwards explains, they reveal as much about the importance of the collector as they do about his wealth.

John Skelton was a poet and tutor to young Henry VIII. In his biting satire, *Colin Clout*, he mocked Cardinal Wolsey for his lavish use of tapestries. But Wolsey was merely following the Tudor fashion and using tapestry to display both his wealth and – by identifying himself with the stories they told – his self-image.

By the time of his downfall in 1529 this man of God had amassed some 600 tapestries. A handful of these still exist and can be found in the Great Watching Chamber today. More importantly for the palace's story, Wolsey's collecting inevitably influenced the young King's taste and when Henry VIII took over Hampton Court, all those tapestries came to him.

Henry's collecting was in another league: in fact, by his death in 1547 he had over 2,000 tapestries, probably the largest collection anywhere. To understand what an achievement this was, we should remember that a set of tapestries to cover a room might take a team of men two years to make. The finest work from the workshops of Brussels could cost up to £3 for a little less than a square yard at a time when a family could live off £5 for a year.

On special occasions or holy days the wardrobe department would hang tapestries throughout the palace, saving the finest, worked with silk and sometimes gold thread, for the King's rooms. An ambassador visiting Wolsey here was impressed to pass through eight rooms all hung with tapestries, which he noted were changed once a week.

Today fewer than 30 tapestries remain from this once great collection. They are astonishing survivors that still give the best impression of how the palace would have looked in Henry's day.

The Triumph of Fame over Death from one of Wolsey's sets of the *Triumphs of Petrarch*. The poet Petrarch's complex moralising poem was popular at court: here Fame deposes Death, surrounded by heroes from history.

Our conservators have a rolling programme for conserving the tapestries and for this reason you may find that particular pieces are not always on display.

In this weaving of the above scene, from the collection of the Victoria & Albert Museum, Wolsey ordered King Henry and himself to be shown amongst the victors.

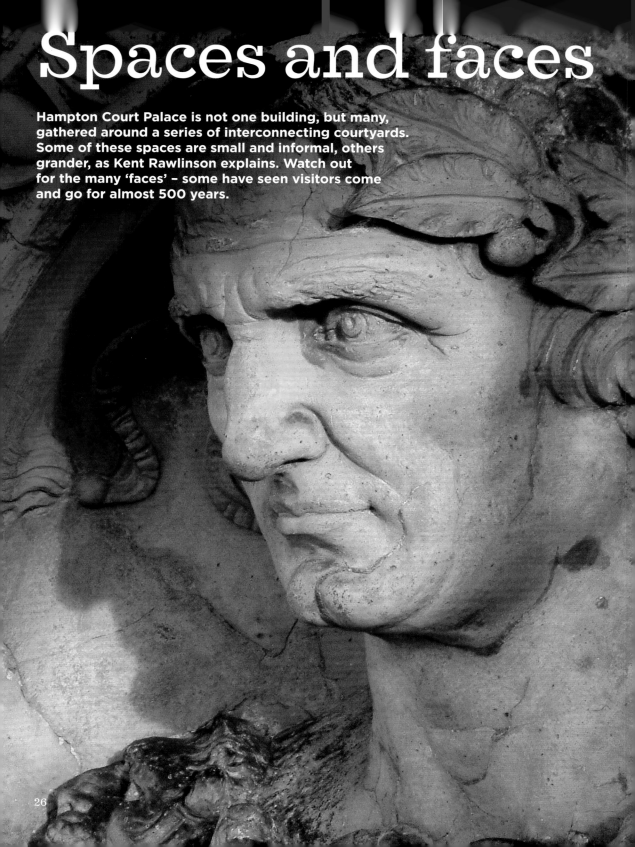

Spaces and faces

Hampton Court Palace is not one building, but many, gathered around a series of interconnecting courtyards. Some of these spaces are small and informal, others grander, as Kent Rawlinson explains. Watch out for the many 'faces' – some have seen visitors come and go for almost 500 years.

The West Front: The outer green court

Wolsey and Henry's guests arrived by river, the fastest and most pleasant route from London. Others who arrived by land entered through the first courtyard, outer green court – that is today's West Front.

Here, builders and craftsmen worked on programme after programme of construction and improvement between 1514 and 1539. Until 1536, this was their work yard. Millions of handmade bricks and tiles, as well as tons of stone, timber and lead were floated by river and landed at 'the Thames' side'. They used vitrified (or burnt) bricks to form the large diaper (criss-cross) patterns which decorate the palace's courtyards.

Wolsey's Great Gatehouse, completed by around 1521, conjured a grand entrance to his palace, dwarfing the surrounding countryside. It reached two storeys higher than today and was topped with elaborate onion domes. Passing over Henry VIII's moat bridge, past his 'king's beasts', and beneath the gaze of two terracotta emperors, we enter the palace's largest courtyard – Base Court.

Naturally only the great and the good entered the palace this way. Servants and other household officers used the other large entrance to the left, Seymour Gate. All the palace's food and day-to-day necessities passed through the archway and into a warren of small courtyards, kitchens and offices.

Roman faces

The archway designed by William Kent in Clock Court is adorned with four Roman emperors, six more of which glare down from the palace's other gatehouses, including Tiberius (left). Wolsey commissioned these terracotta masterpieces from a Florentine sculptor, Giovanni da Maiano, as a statement of his classical learning and cultural sophistication.

Base Court: The lap of luxury

This spacious courtyard provided a cramped, but luxurious home for members and guests of the court. Mostly men, they shared rooms, beds, mattresses and floors.

Behind the many windows are dozens of courtiers' lodgings, each of which had its own fireplace and a 'garderobe' (private toilet). Archaeological excavations here in 2008-9 uncovered many earlier medieval buildings. Our re-creation of Henry VIII's wine fountain stands where the octagonal base of a lost Tudor fountain was revealed.

This was the first courtyard visitors passed through, which explains its French name, *basse* (lower), but it wasn't basic! One of Wolsey's 'gentleman ushers', George Cavendish, recalled entertaining French ambassadors in 1527:

> *... every of them conveyed to his chamber ... having in them great fires and wine ready to refresh them ... a basin and a ewer of silver ... two great pots of silver ... one pot at the least with wine and beer, a bowl or goblet, and a silver pot to drink beer in; a silver candlestick or two ... Thus was every chamber furnished throughout the house.*

This elaborate wine fountain re-creates one made for Henry VIII in 1520. An original painting of it hangs in Young Henry VIII's Story.

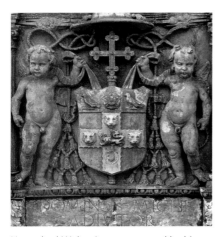

Henry had Wolsey's arms covered by his own, moulded in iron, in 1531. They were rediscovered and restored in the mid-19th century.

The head of Hercules; one of the 46 classical heads that adorn Fountain Court.

Clock Court: Time and tide

Beyond the middle gateway – Anne Boleyn's Gatehouse – is Clock Court, the heart of the palace and named after the extraordinary Astronomical Clock, another famous 'face' in the Tudor building. For over 300 years kings, queens, architects and craftsmen moulded this courtyard to their needs and in their own image.

Wolsey's terracotta coat of arms, held aloft by a pair of angels, survive above the inner side of the entrance to this courtyard.

Dominating the space (to the right of Wolsey's arms) are the tall windows and gilded weather vanes of Henry VIII's Great Hall: the social and ceremonial heart of the Tudor palace.

Opposite stretch out the bright, elegant, columns of Sir Christopher Wren's baroque colonnade, constructed over 150 years later, as a grand entrance to William III's new King's Apartments.

Finally, on the site of Henry VIII and Katherine of Aragon's lavish apartments stands the Cumberland Suite (opposite Wolsey's arms). The architect William Kent designed this in playful mock-Tudor fashion for the young Prince William, Duke of Cumberland, in 1732.

Fountain Court

Henry VIII and his wives had their private apartments here. However, all but Henry's Bayne Tower – comprising his bedroom, bathroom (bayne), study, library and jewel-house – were rebuilt between 1689 and 1694 in the new and dramatic baroque style.

This is the palace's last great courtyard. Behind its formal windows are two sets of royal apartments – one intended for the king, the other for the queen. Behind the upper windows were lodgings for leading servants and courtiers – imagine the views!

William III's wish to be thought a modern-day Hercules is powerfully illustrated throughout these new buildings, not least by painted roundels (now faded, sadly) depicting the story of the hero's tasks in antiquity. A carving of Hercules' lion skin is draped over each round window. Back down to earth, underneath each arch, are delicately carved flowers and royal symbols. Each is topped by the characterful head of a classical god or mythic creature – were some modelled on portraits of those courtiers who once promenaded here?

Henry VIII's Astronomical Clock has watched over this courtyard for almost 500 years. It testifies to the King's passion for scientific learning and architectural exuberance.

Henry VIII's clock incorporates a great bell inherited from the late-medieval manor house that once stood on this site.

Thomas More's son-in-law recalled that:

The kinge... would in the night have him [More] up to his leads [roof] there to discourse within him the diversities, courses and motions and operations of the stars and planets ...

Ring
This stationary outer ring shows the hours of the day.

Outer dial
This large dial rotates annually. It shows the day of the year, the position of the sun in the zodiac, and the date.

Middle dial
This solar dial and pointer rotate daily, telling the time.

Inner dial
This lunar dial rotates monthly. It indicates the phase and visible portion of the moon.

The clock's complex gears and gilded dials depict a medieval world in which the sun orbits the earth. Probably designed by 'the deviser of the king's horologies', Nicolaus Kratzer, a Bavarian, they were made in 1540 by a young Frenchman, Nicholas Oursian. They even indicate the time of high tide; useful for river-travellers such as Henry and his court!

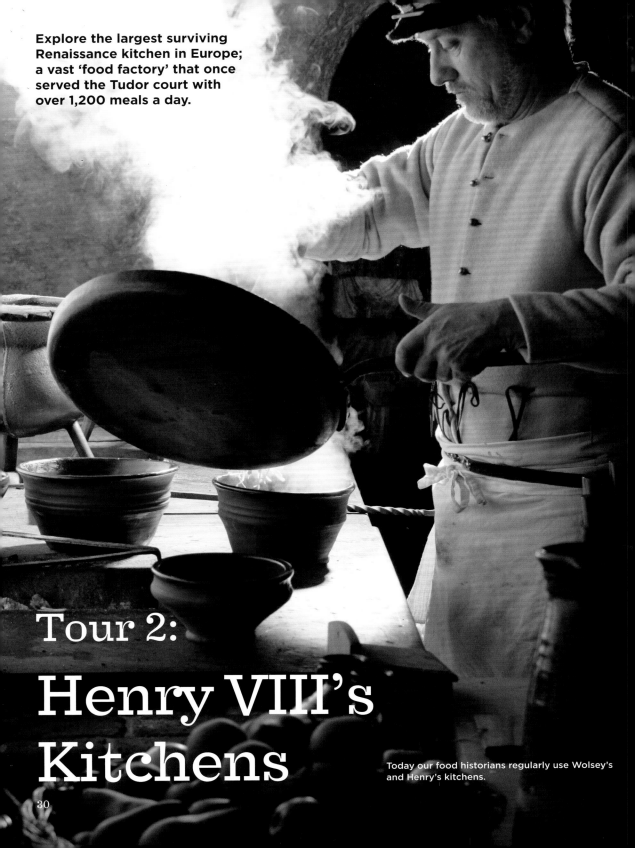

Explore the largest surviving Renaissance kitchen in Europe; a vast 'food factory' that once served the Tudor court with over 1,200 meals a day.

Tour 2:
Henry VIII's Kitchens

Today our food historians regularly use Wolsey's and Henry's kitchens.

The Kitchens today

Even though a large part of Henry VIII's Kitchens has either been taken down or is no longer accessible, you are still able to visit a massive set of kitchens. To help you understand the enormous processing work, the route has been laid out to show how raw food came in one end of the kitchens and out the other as food fit for a royal court. All the replica food and utensils on show are based on research undertaken by our food historians here at the palace. (See below)

Master Carpenter's Court

This large space is big enough to turn a cart around! And with good reason, provisions entered the kitchens through the back gate, down under the arch. The never-ending supply of goods would have been rolling in here daily, to be put into stores, or carried to any of the smaller kitchens by an army of staff.

Fiddling was kept to a minimum by the scrupulous accounting by officials of the Board of the Green Cloth.

The entire kitchens were controlled by the offices above the arch, called the 'Board of the Green Cloth', where officials accounted and paid for all the goods.

Boiling House

This is one of many smaller kitchens that would have been used exclusively for simple preparatory work. Here we have a room put aside for the jointing of meat. Next door (up a small flight of stairs) meat is boiling in the great boiling pot, to go into waiting pies. The pie cases would not have been made here, but brought over from the pastry department.

Fish Court

Ever wanted to stand in a Tudor fridge? Well this is how Fish Court works. A central set of store rooms in the middle of the kitchen complex, it allows for the short-term storage of many raw ingredients. The space is narrow, running north to south so that the sun does not shine here; open to the air so that the stone stores stay nice and cool. We know that the stores on the right as you enter were used for fresh fish.

Historic kitchens team

What started as an annual historic cooking display has become a fascinating ongoing research project. Our team of historians use recipe research to trace the meals eaten at the royal court. To cook the food by authentic means they design reproductions of every kitchen item, from bowls and spoons to cooks' clothing. All of this comes together in their live practical experiments, when food preparation and cookery is carried out in front of visitors, culminating in the serving and eating of a historic meal, in costume, at the end of the day. Visit www.hrp.org.uk for details of forthcoming cookery displays.

The Great Kitchens

This huge room, now divided into three spaces, is the most impressive of the kitchens and the easiest to understand. Originally it was used just for roasting fresh meat, mostly beef, on the spits over the six great fires in this set of rooms.

Later additions to the rooms give us clues to the continued use of the kitchens in later periods. A range of charcoal stoves has been added, as has a small bread oven and a later roasting range.

In the last room of the Great Kitchens you can see a Tudor roasting fire in full glory. Roasting meat on a spit is expensive. Most of the heat goes up the chimney, and you have to pay a man to turn the spit. All part of royal magnificence.

Right: The great roasting fire, an extravagant way to cook meat.

Serving Place

At the end of the Great Kitchens are the hatches through which the finished dishes passed. Another army of servants carried the food to the Great Hall and other chambers. Clerks from the nearby office kept a close eye on the proceedings at this end of the kitchen too, counting the dishes that passed out, and ensuring that the valuable pewter serving dishes, chargers, cups and bowls from the next door store all came back again!

Food, glorious food!

For the Tudor royal court, food was an important way of demonstrating wealth and largesse, particularly when it came to entertaining foreign visitors who would expect to be served treats from all over the world.

The variety of food available at court was staggering. Today we worry about the environmental cost of flying in unseasonal produce; in Tudor times 'food miles' were a sign of status. The more exotic and distant an ingredient, the better. Royal diners enjoyed citrus fruit, almonds and olive oil from the Mediterranean. Dishes were sweetened with sugar from Iraq, and seasoned with pepper and many other spices from Africa and India, and ginger all the way from China.

'Ordinary' Tudor folk would have eaten much the same every day, with some seasonal produce and occasionally some fresh meat and fish, but most of their protein was smoked, salted or cured. By contrast, the Tudor court enjoyed freshly slaughtered, roasted meat every day, and the luxury of being able to chose from a 'physical menu' of tempting dishes.

Wine Cellar

Six hundred meals, twice a day, that's a lot of thirsty people!

To keep the court in beer, wine and ale (water, although safe to drink at the palace, was not very popular) there are a number of cellars in the kitchen complex. Barrels of drink would be delivered to the palace and rolled into the cellars. From here it was poured out into jugs to be served at table. Wine, sent at great expense from Europe, was another status symbol, and was evidently much appreciated!

The Chocolate Kitchen

Don't miss this delicious little kitchen, situated in Fountain Court. George I and George II both adored hot chocolate! Here you can experience chocolate-making first hand, and see how it was served up in royal style.

A royal flush

From the grandest of monarchs to the lowliest of scullions, everyone needs to visit the lavatory. While taking the royal wee was a comfortable and relatively private experience for the king, the lowest members of the Tudor court found the 'conveniences' rather more public, as Chief Curator Lucy Worsley explains.

Main picture: A rare-surviving close stool (portable lavatory) from the palace, probably made for William III.

Room for a little one

Henry VIII had quite a collection of 'close stools': padded stools with a hole in the middle, positioned above a chamber pot. They were similar in design to this rare survivor from the 17th century (left), but the King's own models were far more luxurious. One was padded with black velvet, decorated with swansdown and 'garnished' with 2,000 gilt nails.

In his private lodgings, Henry VIII was attended by the gentlemen of his Privy Chamber, the most senior members of his court. First among them, and taking his title from the close stool itself was the Groom of the Stool, whose important job it was to accompany the King 'when he goeth to make water in his bedchamber'. It's perhaps difficult for us today to appreciate that this was a highly sought-after position, as it allowed such intimate and potentially influential access to the King.

The King's health, and even his bowel movements, were of great interest to everyone at court. Once, when Henry was ill, his doctors gave him a 'glister' or enema, to purge his bowels. In the middle of that night he 'rose to go to the stool, which by working of the pills and glister that his Highness had taken before, had a very fair siege'.

There was no time for the lower members of the court to be coy when they used the Great House of Easement to relieve themselves. Also known as the Common Jakes, this was a 14-seater lavatory for men and boys, positioned over the moat, just south of the Great Gatehouse. Its discharge flowed out into the Thames, where a lock prevented it from re-entering the moat.

The flushing toilet was an invention of late Tudor times, and Britain's first was installed at the Palace of Richmond. But it didn't catch on, and Hampton Court remained desperately short of facilities. Many of the corners of the cloisters and courtyards are still blocked off with 18th-century iron spikes, intended to discourage the Georgian courtiers from taking a leak.

Nights of the bath

The smelliest people in the Tudor palace must have been the scullions, whose job was to remove 'corruption and all uncleaness out of the King's house, which doth engender danger of infection and is very noisome and displeasant unto all noblemen and others'.

Fresh water for drinking and washing kitchen utensils was brought to the palace by a network of underground brick conduits running all the way from a spring on Kingston Hill, but bathing was undertaken only rarely, and with a sense that it might be dangerous.

Henry VIII though, was a frequent user of his very sophisticated bathroom. He constructed a room in the 'Bayne' or bath tower for his bath, which was circular like a barrel cut in half and lined with a linen sheet before being filled with water.

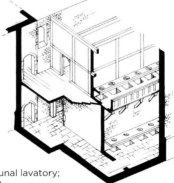

A reconstruction of the communal lavatory; efficient if not exactly discreet!

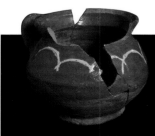

Members of the royal household also used chamberpots like this one which was discovered in excavations. Scientific analysis proved that it still contains traces of Tudor urine. The lodgings of more senior officials, such as those in Base Court, had their own garderobe shafts or built-in lavatories.

William, Mary and Anne

William III (reigned 1689-1702) and Mary II (reigned 1689-94) did more than any other monarchs to reshape the palace as you see it today. And we have Mary's sister Queen Anne (reigned 1702-14) to thank both for the re-modelling of the chapel and the wall paintings by Verrio that decorate the Queen's Drawing Room. But what sort of king and queens were they?

Above: William III and Mary II painted by William Wissing around 1685.

Short and asthmatic, William must at first sight have seemed unimpressive. He was at least 12cm shorter than his English wife Mary, with distinctive, rather than handsome features. William, a single child who never knew his father, had been raised in the Netherlands as a prince with little prospect of ruling. Unsurprisingly perhaps, he was unfriendly, at times even morose. However, in defending his homeland against the French, he had proved himself a natural leader of men.

He has been called the first truly European leader, who fought to keep the balance of power in Europe. In contrast to his uncle James II, he was a devout Protestant with a relatively modest lifestyle, although his private pleasures included hard drinking, gambling and hunting.

Mary, warm-hearted and attractive, was just 15 when she left England in tears for an arranged marriage to her much older Dutch cousin. However, in time she grew to love dour William, in spite of his blatant affair with one of her maids of honour. Although intelligent her education as a princess did not prepare her to rule, and when she accepted her deposed father's throne she was adamant that William would wield royal power. So at the age of 28 she felt ill-suited to run the country when William departed to fight in Ireland. Yet with wise counsel and her own good judgement she flourished. William himself admitted that 'if he left us, the Queen would govern us better'. Her sudden death from smallpox in 1694 left both King and the nation bereft.

Anne shared many of her elder sister Mary's views but was quite different. If Mary was often tactful and persuasive, Anne was shy and stubborn, which sometimes served her well in times of national crisis. Anne detested William, whom she nicknamed Caliban, the monster from Shakespeare's *The Tempest*. William in turn delighted in being spiteful to Anne, whose claim to the throne was greater than his. He once ate a whole plate of new peas in front of her without offering her any.

As queen, Anne was far more popular with the public. However, she shied away from court life and was happiest hunting, which she did in a carriage because of her poor health. She married the handsome Prince George of Denmark, and they had 17 children. Tragically, none survived to adulthood. Anne died knowing that her family's reign was finally ended.

Above: A popular broadsheet print celebrating William and Mary's acceptance of the joint crown at Westminster in 1689.

Left: In spite of ill health and none of her many children surviving, Queen Anne was popular and successful. By Sir Godfrey Kneller.

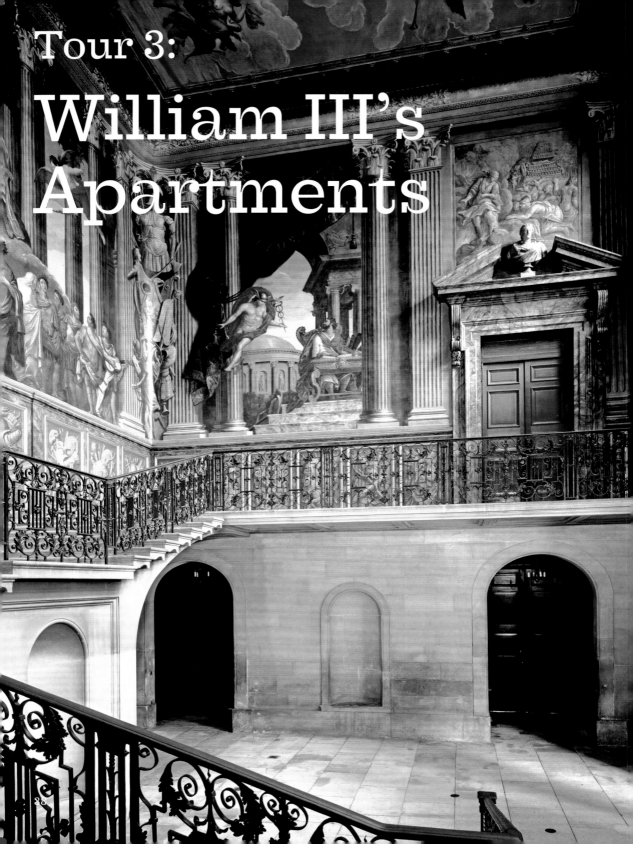

Tour 3:
William III's Apartments

These lofty baroque rooms were designed for meeting the King with state ceremony. Following protocol used as far back as Henry VIII, access to each successive room was granted according to a person's increasing status, under the watchful eye of the guards, ushers and waiters. With every step nearer His Majesty's presence the rooms become richer, yet more intimate.

The grand South Front of William and Mary's new palace was designed and built by Sir Christopher Wren and his clerk of works, Nicholas Hawksmoor, with almost indecent haste. In fact the main wall collapsed during the winter of 1689, causing death and injury and almost losing Wren his job. After the Queen's death five years later work stopped and the King's attention returned to war in Europe. Around 1699 William eventually found time and money to finish and furnish these empty rooms, which the court then enjoyed briefly for two years before his untimely death in 1702.

The King's Staircase and Guard Chamber

King William wanted to inspire awe in his visitors as they climbed up to the *piano nobile* – the principal floor. He employed the Italian painter, Antonio Verrio, to create the illusion of a great Roman hall as the setting for the story of a competition between the commanders Alexander the Great and Julius Caesar, who vied for a seat beneath the gods' banquet on the ceiling above. No doubt that the warring William identified with the victor, Alexander, but contemporaries would have understood a second message: that the Roman Catholic James II had been defeated by a Protestant leader.

This military theme continues into the Guard Chamber, where the King's gunsmith, John Harris, created the room's architectural décor out of 2,850 pieces of arms and armour. This large and important collection of 17th and 18th-century weapons would have been a potent reminder of the real threat of war and rebellion in 1700.

Here the Yeomen of the Guard kept watch to deter 'mean or ordinary persons'. You can still see their *partisans*, a type of pike.

Above: The canopy of state in the King's Presence Chamber.

Left: The King's Staircase, with murals by Antonio Verrio.

39

Above: Detail from the *Triumph of Hercules* tapestry, made for Henry VIII and chosen to hang in the Presence Chamber by William III, who liked to identify with the Greek hero.

Left: Kneller's great portrait of William III on horseback, painted for the King's Presence Chamber.

Right: The Privy Chamber, reflected in one of its huge engraved pier glasses.

The King's Presence Chamber

The first reception room was where the wider members of court would meet the King, sitting beneath a richly upholstered canopy above a dais (low platform). By William's day its use had rather fossilised and most visitors were likely to doff their hats to an empty chair, opposite Sir Godfrey Kneller's imposing equestrian portrait, which was specially painted for this room. The King took a personal interest in the art shown at his palace and hung some of Henry VIII's finest tapestries in this apartment. The large silver chandelier is another mark of William's wealth – even though he was often short of ready money.

The King's Eating Room

Dining rooms were still something of a novelty in England when the Dutch-born William III came to rule. He also disliked the traditional, but stuffy, ceremony of dining in front of a crowd. So this room may only have been used on a few formal occasions, when tables and food were brought in along a winding route from the old kitchens. The wheat ears and fruit in Grinling Gibbons's limewood carvings above the fireplace are a sign of the room's use (below).

Grinling Gibbons's famous naturalistic wood carving sometimes betrays a room's original function.

The King's Privy Chamber

This grand saloon, with the second chair of
state and another original and rare canopy,
would have hosted formal receptions, such as
ambassadors with their large entourages. In
Tudor times the Privy Chamber was actually
fairly private, but by 1700 everyone wanted
to be there. Here are two more of Henry VIII's
old tapestries, scenes from the *Story of
Abraham*: six more of these are usually in
the Great Hall. William's Stuart ancestor,
Elizabeth of Bohemia, by Gerrit van Honthorst,
gazes from the mantelpiece to remind guests
of William's legitimate rule in England. In the
evenings the superb, gilded candle stands,
and the tables (these are replicas) with their
extravagantly large mirrors would have
shimmered and dazzled by candlelight.

The Withdrawing Room, Great Bedchamber and Little Bedchamber

Formerly the most exclusive receiving room, the Withdrawing Room marked the boundary between the more public rooms and the separate realm of the bedchambers, where the king was attended by Gentlemen of the Bedchamber. In the Great Bedchamber the king might receive senior courtiers and ministers while dressing, a French royal custom, known as the *levée*. The bedchamber is appropriately one of the most sumptuous rooms in the palace. Next door is the Little Bedchamber, where William could retire in relative privacy.

The King's Closet and back stairs

In this closet the King could conduct his important business, one to one and in comfort. Here is his walnut desk and long-case clock by Daniel Quare, that only needs winding once a year: an extraordinary piece of technology for the day. The jib doors lead to his original close stool (portable lavatory) and the back stairs. The Groom of the Stool was a senior courtier who not only ran the Bedchamber department, but also had to personally attend the king on his 'stool'. William or his favourite courtier of the time, the Earl of Albemarle, could use these stairs to slip away to their private rooms downstairs.

The Great Bedchamber was William III's inner sanctum; access was strictly controlled by the Groom of the Stool. Those privileged to attend while the king was dressed were kept at a suitable distance behind a gilded rail.

The King's Private Dining Room laid out for dessert. On the walls hang Kneller's *Hampton Court Beauties* - ladies of Queen Mary's court.

King William's private apartments

William preferred his own company or to be with a few friends on this private floor. In the East, Middle and West closets he would enjoy some of his favourite Old Master paintings, gaming, write letters and even sleep. He had yet another bed in the Middle Closet. Beyond is the Orangery, which was used to over-winter citrus trees. The windows look out onto William's Privy Garden. The patterns of its formal paths and parterres share much in common with the designs for the furnishings of the apartments. The five Italian marble statues were bought for this garden, but in recent years have been brought indoors.

At the far end are the Private Drawing and Dining Rooms where the King would meet his closest acquaintances and drink heavily during dinner. After Mary's death he moved her set of paintings, known as the *Hampton Court Beauties*, by Kneller, to his new little dining room. The buffet was used to show off the monarch's wealth: today it displays copies of royal and noble silver plate.

Fire!

On Easter Day 1986 a terrible fire started in a grace-and-favour apartment above the King's Apartments, bringing down the ceilings here and in the Cartoon Gallery. Buried among charred timbers and molten lead were the Canopy of State, exquisite limewood carvings and the superb, rare chandelier made from rock crystal. A heroic salvage effort was followed by several years of painstaking conservation and restoration. An army of craftsmen and women re-used as much as possible and missing pieces of the building and objects were skilfully re-made.

Built by Christopher Wren on the site of Queen Anne Boleyn's apartments these rooms really came to life with the arrival in 1714 of George, Prince of Wales, the heir to the throne and his wife, Princess Caroline. When George I returned in the summers to Hanover he reluctantly agreed for them to represent him in England as he had no queen, and they entertained here in lavish style.

Tour 4:
The Georgian Story

Meet the Hanoverians

George I (reigned 1714-27) Britain's first Hanoverian king was not too thrilled at the prospect of ruling England and returned to his beloved homeland in Germany as often as he could. A cold and rather dull individual, George did not even have a vivacious queen as a foil to his character, having divorced, then locked up his wife for adultery many years before.

George II (reigned 1727-60) Brave but boorish, George II pursued an obsessive love of all things military and had a terrible relationship with both his father and his son. As Prince of Wales he and his lively wife Caroline set up a rival – and more popular – court at Hampton Court when George I first returned to Hanover. Tension culminated in a huge family row. The royal couple were barred from court for several years and cruelly separated from their children.

Queen Caroline (Queen Consort 1727-37) Unlike her husband and father-in-law, Caroline was cultivated and sociable, gathering about her a lively circle at court. Her close friends included the Prime Minister, Sir Robert Walpole and the waspish Lord Hervey, the Vice Chamberlain.

Frederick, Prince of Wales (born 1707, died 1751) George and Caroline loathed their eldest son and heir, Frederick (the father of the future GIII). They preferred their much younger son William, Duke of Cumberland. Frederick was a lively personality but a constant thorn in the side of his parents.

The Queen's Staircase and Honthorst's painting of Charles I as Apollo (see page 57).

The Queen's Staircase

In 1734, Queen Caroline invited her favourite architect and designer, William Kent, to redecorate the stairs. Although William III had built grand marble steps with their wrought iron balustrade by the master smith, Jean Tijou, the walls had been left plain. Kent's Roman-inspired setting includes a homage to the queen, whom he compares to the ancient goddess Britannia.

The Queen's Guard Chamber and Presence Chamber

Prince George and Princess Caroline of Wales turned to Vanbrugh, the baroque architect who briefly ousted the old Christopher Wren from favour, to finish these rooms in 1717. He commemorated the Yeoman of the Guard who kept watch in the guardroom with the monumental – but rather comic – figures who support the massive chimneypiece. Their job was to make sure that only those known to the court and suitably attired were allowed inside. In the Presence Chamber there was originally a canopy above the chairs where the Prince and Princess would receive in state. Today the room is hung with historic portraits, introducing the Hanoverians and their ancestors.

45

The Public Dining Room

It was essential for the new royal family to be accessible and show off the magnificence of their court. George I detested formality but he was persuaded to take up dining in public after his son and daughter-in-law finished these rooms to entertain in royal fashion, directly in competition. So many people came to view the splendour of the royal table that special barriers had to be introduced to hold them back. George had a preference for German home cooking as well as French dishes, and he built a new 'German Kitchen' to replace the old Tudor kitchens. The contemporary table display reflects the British and Hanoverian royal symbols which also make a unique appearance in Grinling Gibbons' huge sculpted chimneypiece of 1717. The baroque 17th and early-18th century paintings continue this room's theme of dining and entertaining.

The Queen's Privy Chamber

This room was furnished by George and Caroline, representing George I, to hold formal audiences together, seated on chairs of state beneath the original crimson damask canopy. When George I travelled to Hanover in 1716 envoys flocked here to pay their respects to the Prince and Princess in his place and the room would have been crowded with both English and German courtiers. An old portrait of Anne of Denmark, James I's queen, by Van Somer, was chosen by the Hanoverians to remind the English of their shared ancestry. The original great rock crystal chandelier and gilt wood mirrors added sparkle to these occasions when everyone glittered in their fine court clothes.

The Queen's Privy Chamber, where the Prince and Princess of Wales would receive courtiers jointly in the absence of George I.

The Queen's Gallery remains little changed from 1737, the year Queen Caroline died.

The Queen's Drawing Room

The grandest room for entertaining was the Drawing Room, created between 1703 and 1705 by George I's predecessor, Queen Anne, to hold the bustling afternoon receptions known as 'drawing rooms' which became fashionable around this time. Although Anne and her Danish husband, Prince George, are celebrated in Verrio's wall paintings along with the rise of British naval power, it was George and Caroline who made the most of its size and location, which emphasised their position at the heart of the palace. The spectacular view reinforces this message, as you look down the 1,200m Long Water canal and across the baroque landscape which was laid out by King Charles II in the 1660s, in competition with his great rival, Louis XIV of France. In the Drawing Room, courtiers would have stood stiffly in 'the circle' to meet the royal couple or gambled at cards, perhaps listening to music, during informal evening occasions.

The Queen's Bedchamber

The ceiling painting of this room by Sir James Thornhill gives a snapshot of the Hanoverian royal family when painted in 1715. Prince George and Princess Caroline look down on their great state bed made in the same year, where they would have held morning receptions called *levers*, under the eyes of King George I and their absent son, Prince Frederick. The central scene is the ancient Roman story of Aurora, goddess of the Dawn, who abducted her mortal love Cephalus: a moralising story of marital fidelity for the notoriously unfaithful Hanoverians.

There would have been a portable rail around the bed to separate the seated royal couple from their audience and its place is taken today by a very rare

Queen Caroline's State Bed, with her father-in-law George I looking down.

gilded bed rail of the early 17th century, which was used by Charles II and George I who both admired such French court fashions.

The Queen's Gallery

The Gallery marked the beginning of the private royal apartments, where the royal family could converse and exercise when the weather prevented them enjoying the gardens. The room was first used by William III, who had the beautiful chimneypiece put here in memory of his late queen, Mary II. Her Delftware flowerpots also remain and were much to the taste of Queen Caroline, who added the unusual stools and probably the tapestries showing the History of Alexander the Great, a flattering allusion for her husband George II, who was the last British king to fight in battle.

The Queen's Closet

This room may be periodically closed.
Queen Mary II planned this little room as a luxuriously decorated study but died suddenly in 1694 before it was finished. William III turned it into a memorial to his queen and the room was hung with her embroideries for years to come. These were designed by the influential baroque architect, Daniel Marot.

The Ladies of the Bedchamber's Room

This important room leads to both Queen Caroline's private apartments and the backstairs, where her servants had lodgings. Here her bedchamber women, such as George II's mistress, Henrietta Howard, would wait on her from dawn until bedtime in a dreary round of personal duties. They even slept here, in a tiny mezzanine floor room above so that they were always on hand.

The Queen's Private Apartments

These intimate rooms were where Princess, later Queen, Caroline, did her everyday living. They are shown today as they would have been during the time after 1727 when she used them exclusively as Queen Consort to George II. She would only share them with her close servants such as the Vice Chamberlain, Lord Hervey or invited guests like her good friend, the first minister Robert Walpole.

The Queen's Private Drawing Room

This room is laid out with a Meissen tea service (from Germany), and game of *quadrille*, a popular card game in the 18th century which was often played for high stakes. Like all these rooms it has a tiered chimneypiece where Caroline could show off her collection of exotic Chinese and Japanese porcelain. The Queen and her friends would play cards most evenings as they gossiped about the people at court.

The Queen's Closet was planned as a study for a former occupant of these rooms, Queen Mary II.

Queen Caroline's Private Bedchamber with its beautiful angel bed which belonged to her minister, Lord Townsend.

Queen Caroline with her youngest, and favourite son William, Duke of Cumberland, who grew up to be known as 'The Butcher of Culloden'.

The Queen's Private Bedchamber, Dressing Room, Bathroom and Closet

This was where the Queen actually slept and according to etiquette, would invite the King to sleep with her when required, although he preferred to spend more time with his mistresses. Uniquely, the doors can be bolted from the inside to ensure privacy from servants, but released in the morning by pulling on a cord from the bedside. Caroline's own bed has been lost but has been replaced with a contemporary 'angel bed' with its top hanging from the ceiling. In the room beyond the Queen, seated and wearing a shift, would be bathed by her bedchamber women. Then hours would be spent at her *toilette*, preparing her face and hair for the day. Caroline was unusually enthusiastic about washing for her time. Next door she had one of the few water closets (lavatories) and a cupboard for all her exquisite linen.

The Queen's Private Dining Room and Sideboard Room

The Queen could slip out of the great drawing room next door and enjoy supper here in private, perhaps with her daughters or favourite younger son, William. Around them she hung Van de Velde's sea battles from the Anglo-Dutch war, a patriotic choice of paintings. Prince Frederick was probably rarely invited: Caroline's relationship with her elder son, the Prince of Wales, was very bad and they fell out for the last time shortly before her death in 1737 when he defied her and rushed his wife away from Hampton Court one night during childbirth. As a result he was unwelcome at the palace.

The Queen's Private Oratory

The cherubs' heads in the lantern made by Grinling Gibbons' carvers reveal that this room was used for private prayers by the Lutheran Queen Caroline. She was a devout woman and very interested in theology. The story here ends with Caroline's premature death, which took place at St James's Palace after a prolonged and painful illness. Afterwards George II took little further interest in his summer palace of Hampton Court.

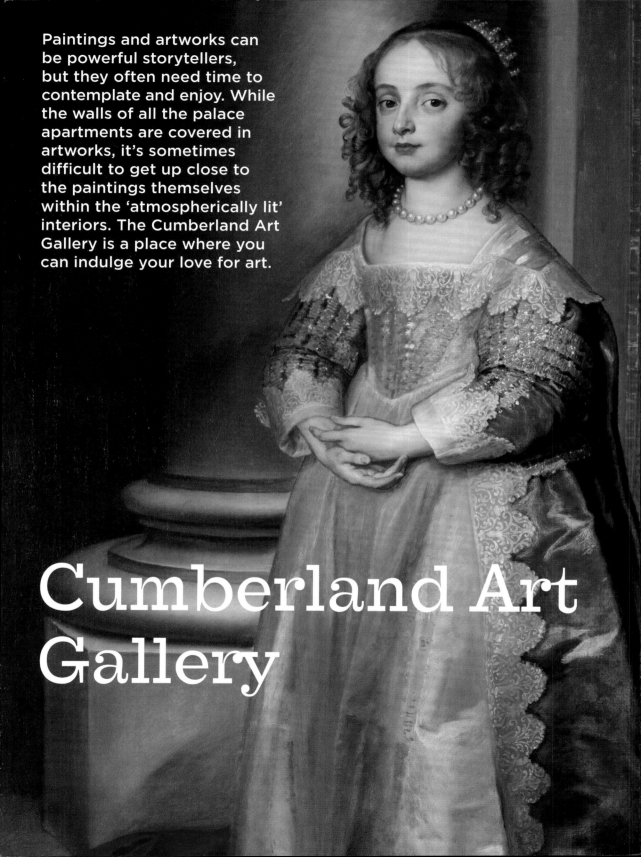

Paintings and artworks can be powerful storytellers, but they often need time to contemplate and enjoy. While the walls of all the palace apartments are covered in artworks, it's sometimes difficult to get up close to the paintings themselves within the 'atmospherically lit' interiors. The Cumberland Art Gallery is a place where you can indulge your love for art.

Cumberland Art Gallery

The Cumberland Art Gallery takes up four remaining rooms of what was once the apartment of William Augustus, Duke of Cumberland, the younger and favourite son of King George II. The architect William Kent designed and decorated the interiors for the young Prince between 1731-32; he embraced the latest Palladian fashion (named after the Italian architect Andrea Palladio) but was also fascinated by the surviving Tudor decoration at the palace. The elaborate plaster ceiling of the Duke's Presence Chamber looks back to Hampton Court's Tudor past and is a very early example of the Gothic Revival style.

The rooms are works of art themselves and are now a fitting home for a rotating display of paintings that will help you further explore royal tastes and the lives of those who lived and died at Hampton Court. The artworks on display range from Tudor and Renaissance portraits to Georgian landscapes and baroque allegories, stories from the Bible or mythology retold for court audiences and often loaded with implicit messages about royal power.

Left: Anthony Van Dyck, *Princess Mary Stuart* (detail). Court artists like Van Dyck worked directly for the royal family. This portrait, of the 6-year-old daughter of Charles I, is a statement of royal wealth (the expensive lace, pearls and golden damask) and dynastic strength (the great stone column) but it is also a wonderfully personal portrait of a little girl with her hands clasped uncertainly in front of her silver apron. Van Dyck worked hard to create the right expressive gesture: if you look closely you can see how the artist changed his mind in his depiction of Mary's hands.

Right: Rembrandt, *Self-portrait in a Flat Cap, 1642* This is the self-confident image of the greatest artist of the 17th-century Netherlands. Rembrandt painted himself over 40 times, essays of artistic self-expression that trace his life and career over 50 years. This portrait shows him as a successful man of the world, aged 36, as yet untroubled by the difficulties of his later life.

Above: Canaletto, *The Grand Canal from the Salute towards the Carità*. Canaletto's 'postcard' views of 1720s Venice were in great demand in the 18th century; as mementoes for those that had travelled across Europe as part of the 'Grand Tour' and also for those that never went. George III didn't make it to Venice, but bought this set of 12 paintings from Joseph Smith, the English Consul, who assembled a great collection of 'modern' Venetian art.

Right: Artemisia Gentileschi, *Self-portrait as 'Painting'*. This is one of the most arresting paintings hanging at the palace and one of the most revealing portraits of a 17th-century woman. Artemisia has depicted herself both as a working artist and as 'La Pittura', a female muse representing the idea of painting. It is a wonderfully dynamic portrait, with Artemisia lost in the moment, her hair tied back and dishevelled, her body contorted as she devotes all her concentration to the canvas.

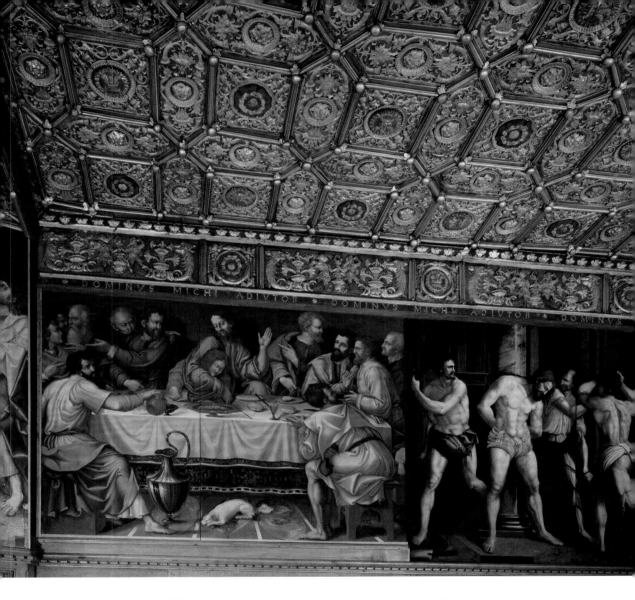

The Wolsey Closet

Buried within the Cumberland Suite is an unexpected artistic treasure. The Wolsey Closet is a heavily restored fragment of Henry VIII's private chambers, almost all of which have been destroyed. It is also something of a puzzle. Although much of the wood and leather maché ceiling is from Henry VIII's time, the linenfold panelling and other pieces of decoration were introduced when this space was opened to the public in 1889. The decorated frieze, probably from another part of Hampton Court, is linked to Cardinal Wolsey by his Latin motto,

Dominus miche adiutor (The Lord is my helper) while the painted scenes from the Passion of Christ have been assembled from at least two different 15th and 16th-century sets of paintings. The Wolsey Closet nonetheless creates a sense of the intimacy and richness of a small 16th-century closet, a private retreat where Henry VIII could relax, read or entertain close companions. The painted panels also show us the astonishing quality of work that Henry acquired to decorate his palaces and how such art was displayed in the 16th century.

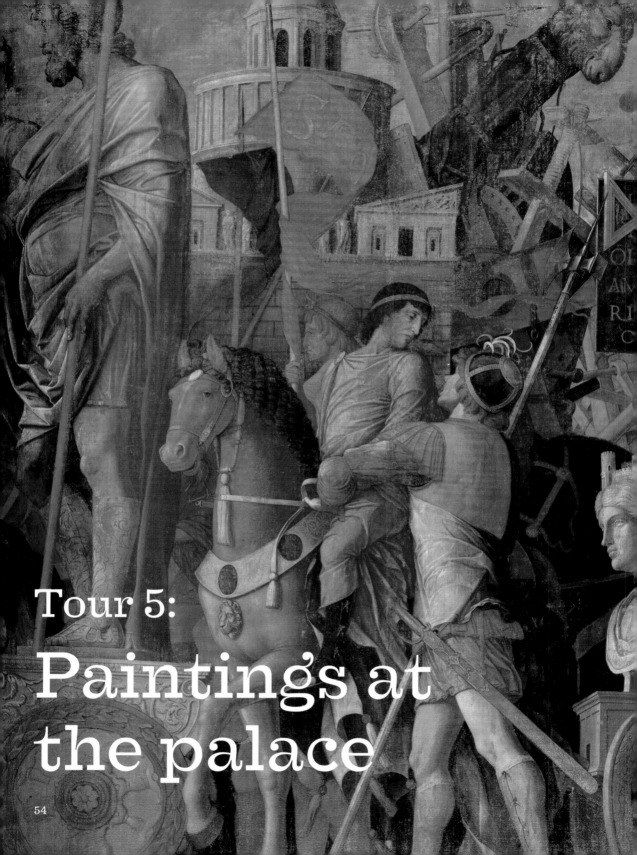

Tour 5:
Paintings at the palace

The Royal Collection, held in trust by Her Majesty Queen Elizabeth II for her successors and the nation, is one of the largest and finest of its kind in the world. Many of its greatest treasures, dating from the 16th to the 18th centuries, can be seen among the thousands of works from the Collection on show at Hampton Court. Displays change from time to time as works from the Collection are frequently lent temporarily to exhibitions elsewhere. This is a short introduction to some of the highlights. To explore the collection in depth visit www.royalcollection.org.uk

Must see:
The Triumphs of Caesar by Andrea Mantegna
Where to see them:
The Lower Orangery

These nine huge canvases, painted between 1484 and 1505, caused a sensation when they appeared on the walls of the palace of Gianfrancesco Gonzaga, the Marquis of Mantua. Before this, people struggled to imagine what Ancient Rome looked like, although Roman literature and history were very fashionable. Suddenly, you could be transported back in time, with Julius Caesar's triumphal procession rolling past. These paintings are full of noise and detail but everything is arranged with an ingenious worm's eye perspective. Mantegna had spent years researching the historical details and his *Triumphs* became, for a time, the most famous paintings in Europe. Mantegna was the first truly 'famous' artist.

Left: *The Triumphs of Caesar* canvas II, *The Triumphal Carts*

The *Triumphs of Caesar* have been at the palace since 1630. They were purchased by Charles I from the Gonzaga family. In this, the second of the nine canvases, Mantegna shows us some of the vast wealth seized by Caesar from his enemies and displayed for his adoring public as he marches through the streets of Rome. These paintings are grand statements about power and success, and Caesar was venerated by later world leaders who sought to emulate his victories.

Above: *The Battle of the Spurs* was painted to celebrate Henry VIII's magnificent 1513 campaign against the French armies of Louis XII. You can see Henry on his horse right in the centre. It's a nice image, but pure fiction. In reality, Henry took no part in the battle at all.

Must see:
The Battle of the Spurs
Where to see it:
'Young Henry VIII's Story', The Wolsey Rooms

Henry VIII sought to emulate Julius Caesar and achieve fame and immortality on the battlefield. The story of Henry's achievements can be traced in art through rare survivals from the Tudor period on display at Hampton Court today. Paintings like *The Battle of the Spurs* and *The Field of the Cloth of Gold* are in their own way the Tudor 'Triumphs of Henry VIII', commissioned to tell the story of a great general who attempted to rewrite the map of Europe in war and in peace.

Must see:
The Liberal Arts are presented to Charles I
by Gerrit van Honthorst
Where to see it:
The Queen's Staircase

Charles I was a true connoisseur, assembling a grand art collection that reflected his self-image as a magnificent monarch and a grand artistic patron. Completed in 1628, Honthorst's painting shows Charles as Apollo, the Greek god of the sun and of all the civilised arts, enthroned alongside Queen Henrietta Maria, playing the role of the goddess Diana. The controversial royal favourite, the Duke of Buckingham, here in the guise of Mercury, leads the assembled throng of suitably deferential figures representing the arts and the sciences.

Must see:

Pythagoras advocating vegetarianism
by Sir Peter Paul Rubens and
Frans Snyders

Where to see it:

The Public Dining Room

The Baroque style in art was a visceral
explosion of flesh and colour. Rubens
was its grand master but here he has
collaborated with his friend Snyders, an
expert in painting still-lifes, to produce
an intricately observed banquet of
foodstuffs designed to assault our
senses and appetites. The painting is
also, like so many storytelling artworks
from this period, a complicated
philosophical essay. Pythagoras was the
legendary leader of a sect that thought
flesh-eating barbaric; he argued for a
return to a mythic 'Golden Age' when
the fruits of the earth were enjoyed
without labour or bloodshed.

Above: Rubens and Snyders worked on this painting together
in the 1620s. Snyders painted the fruit and vegetables first, and
then handed the canvas over to Rubens, who was careful not
to paint over his friend's work as he completed the figures.

Below: Honthorst's painting conjures up the theatrical
decadence of a Stuart court masque. These spectacular
productions involved music, dancing, elaborate special
effects (including miraculous 'floating clouds') and
opportunities for the court to dress up – and dress down:
semi-nudity was not uncommon!

William III's riverside retreat was a place to entertain friends amidst Verrio's somewhat racy depictions of the loves of the Gods drawn from Ovid's Metamorphoses. In 1864, a new tenant, Mrs Bailey, protested to the Lord Chamberlain that the 'large undressed figures ... should either be draped or clouded in some way to render them appropriate

Left: Of all of Lely's languorous subjects, Barbara was the most notorious: lover of Charles II, and mother of (at least) five of his illegitimate children. She was handsomely rewarded with titles and property and even became Keeper of Hampton Court with her own splendid set of apartments.

Above: The paintings hanging in the Cartoon Gallery today are copies composed from Raphael's originals in 1697.

Must see:
Antonio Verrio's wall and ceiling paintings
Where to see them:
The Banqueting House; the King's State Apartments

In the later years of the 1600s, it became fashionable to follow the European example of decorating a whole room with elaborate murals. These were both splendid and extravagant works of art, and cultural or political messages about the wonderful achievements of monarchy.

Verrio painted five rooms at Hampton Court, for William III and afterwards Queen Anne. You can explore all of these for yourself, from the complex justification for William's 'Glorious Revolution' that spans the King's Staircase, to the intimate and personal *Mars asleep in the lap of Venus* of the King's Little Bedchamber.

Must see:
Peter Lely's *Windsor Beauties*
Where to see them:
The Communication Gallery

This series of portraits was collected in the 1660s by Anne Hyde, the first wife of the future James II. The subjects represent some of the most important women at the court of Charles II. Surrounded by an atmosphere of libidinous debauchery, encouraged by the King, some attracted gossip and scandal and one or two did have affairs with members of the inner royal circle. Lely's sleepy-eyed evocations of beauty capture the spirit of the times.

Must see:
The Cartoon Gallery

This is one of the very first 'picture galleries' in Britain, built to display one of the great treasures of the Royal Collection – Raphael's set of 'cartoons' (preparatory drawings) for the great tapestry series, The Acts of the Apostles, commissioned for the Sistine Chapel in the Vatican. The Cartoons were purchased by Charles I and are now on loan to the Victoria & Albert Museum.

In the corner, something stirs...

No visit to Hampton Court is complete without feeling a few shivers down your spine, whispers Sarah Kilby.

There is a woman running towards the Chapel Royal. She is no more than a teenager, lithe and pretty. Her eyes are wild with fear and her breath comes in sobs as she tries to move faster, slowed by the rich velvet of her flowing skirts and heavy jewellery. If she can only reach the King at prayer, surely he will look once more on her beauty and youth and be moved to pity?

But Queen Catherine is dragged away by guards; she is already doomed to die, accused of adultery. The furious King, deep in his devotions, remains deaf to her screams for mercy; desperate cries that we can imagine so well centuries later, as we wander through the 'Haunted Gallery', half-hoping for a glimpse of the legendary ghost of Catherine Howard, executed for treason and screaming through eternity.

As warders since Victorian times have known, there's nothing like a good ghost story to draw the crowds. Thousands of visitors to the palace continue to have their spines enjoyably tingled, especially when lights are low and there's a certain chill in the air.

Numerous alleged sightings of tragic Catherine Howard and other famous resident wraithes such as the 'Grey Lady' – Sybil Penn, wet nurse to Edward VI - have ensured that Hampton Court Palace remains on the UK's 'Most Haunted' list. The discovery of two skeletons in 1871 in shallow graves, together with other inexplicable sounds and sightings in grace-and-favour apartments add to the mystery.

Even the most level-headed of staff at the palace mention areas of the palace where something is 'not as it should be'. On dark winter evenings, one of the surveyors will not linger alone in a certain corner of Fountain Court, having often heard 'a slight rustle' at the point where Tudor stone merges with baroque palace. Others working late in the evening have seen fleeting glimpses of unexplained figures and heard retreating footsteps, or struggled with unlocked doors that suddenly jam, as if they were being pulled by a mysterious force.

Ghostbusters

In May 2000, the noted psychologist Richard Wiseman conducted an experiment at Hampton Court Palace to investigate whether ghosts really were 'all in the mind'. He asked volunteers to describe themselves as either 'believers' or 'non-believers' in the paranormal and asked people in both groups to record any unusual experiences as they wandered around. As you might expected, 'believers' reported more spooky sensations overall, but interestingly, many participants recorded more unusual incidents in the same places – the Haunted Gallery and the Georgian Rooms, whether or not they had prior knowlege of the legends. This suggests that something is happening, but exactly what is still unclear....

Spook or fluke?

This CCTV picture of a ghostly figure, captured apparently flinging open a fire door at the palace, attracted international media attention in October 2003. The doors flew open with great force on three consecutive days, with the ghostly figure making his (?) starring appearance on the second. No living soul has ever come forward to admit responsibility, and security staff remain baffled...

A typical postcard of 'The Hampton Court Ghost' to thrill Victorian visitors. How dare you suggest it is faked!

Tour 6:
The Palace Gardens

Begin an enjoyable wander around the beautiful palace grounds at the East Front, as you step out into one of the most instantly recognisable gardens in England. The Gardens Exhibition, situated through the Gardens Shop on the East Front, explains more about the fascinating history of these gardens.

The Great Fountain Garden

Formerly part of Henry VIII's hunting park, this area was designed by Daniel Marot in 1689 as an elaborate formal garden with 1.8m obelisk yew trees and holly globes, edged in box and punctuated by gravelled avenues and 13 fountains. The central fountain of this arrangement survives as do the yew trees, which grew to their present height during Lancelot Capability Brown's tenure of the gardens in the mid-18th century, when he refused to prune them into unnatural shapes. Pruning was resumed in the early 20th century resulting in the present topiary giants.

This postcard view shows the north end of the Broad Walk, c1920.

The Broad Walk

The half-mile Broad Walk is bordered on the palace side by 2m wide herbaceous borders, progressively re-planted to pioneering designs devised in the early 1920s by Hampton Court's curator and publicist, Ernest Law.

The restored Privy Garden, which was opened by The Prince of Wales in 1995.

The Privy Garden

This area of the garden has always been the monarch's own private plot. Henry VIII's garden was laid out in small patterned squares above which stood heraldic beasts on poles, their golden standards fluttering in the breeze. To either side of these squares raised walkways were dotted with towers providing views into the hunting park. At the river end of the garden a banqueting house stood on a mound, around which spiralled a path, like a giant snail's shell, hedged with a trail of sweet-smelling shrubs. Beyond lay the great watergate, a substantial brick building, where the royal barge docked.

The garden today is a restoration of William III's Privy Garden of 1702. It is a cut parterre with 1.8m pyramid yews and round-headed holly trees interspersed with extravagant flowering spring bulbs and summer annuals, edged with box. On a hot day it is delightful to walk through the hornbeam bower, an outdoor cathedral, cool and vast.

The garden is bordered at the river end by an exuberantly decorated iron screen. This was designed and built by Jean Tijou, a French master blacksmith whose work is found throughout the palace. William III expressed his personal approval for this astounding work of art, which allowed him to see glimpses of the river through its gilded iron foliage.

Below: The gilded central cipher of a panel of the Tijou Screen portraying the harp of Ireland. Other panels show the monogram of William and Mary, the garter emblem and designs representing England, Scotland and France.

Turn the page for your guide to all the contrasting areas of our famous gardens from the ancient Great Vine on the South Front round to the gloriously scented Rose Garden to the west of the palace.

1. Great Fountain Garden (see p62)

2. The Broad Walk (see p63)

3. The Privy Garden (see p63)

4. The Banqueting House

This was built and used by King William III as an after-dinner retreat. It contains wall paintings by Verrio, many showing flowers which bloomed in the palace gardens of the early 18th century.

5. The Pond Garden

In the 16th century, the sunken compartments of Henry VIII's ponds were stocked with fish for the palace kitchens but by 1690 the ponds had been drained. Queen Mary II found the sheltered south-facing gardens an ideal place to house the collection of exotic plants she brought with her from the Netherlands. Today the gardeners make a splash with spring and summer bedding.

6. The Lower Orangery Garden

A newly restored garden in front of the Orangery allows a view in summer of Queen Mary's exotics as they were set out in her day. Some of them are in the attractive blue and white decorated pots, of the type ordered from Delft. These tender plants would have been over-wintered in the Orangery behind, which now houses the great *Triumphs of Caesar* by Mantegna.

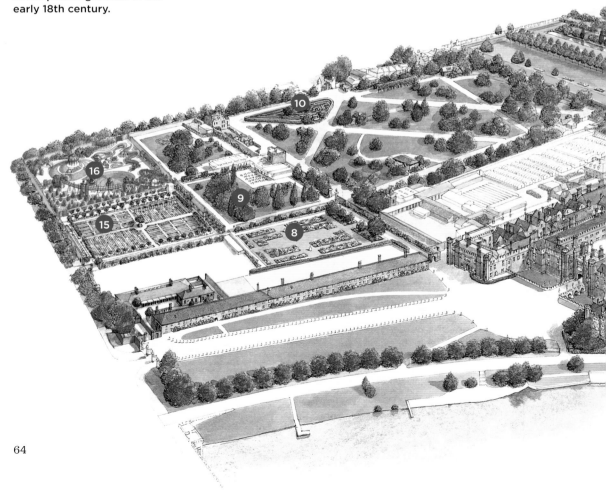

7. The Great Vine

At the end of this walk is a glass-house almost filled with the largest vine in the world, planted by Lancelot Capability Brown in 1768. By the early 20th century, 280,000 visitors a year queued to see this unique Black Hamburg specimen.

8. The Rose Garden

This ever-popular walled garden was once William III's kitchen garden.

9. The Tiltyard Gardens

The Tiltyard tower - where the restaurant now stands - is the survivor of five such towers created for viewing Henry VIII's tournaments, although jousting had already been replaced by the gentler royal pastimes of bowling and tennis.

10. The Wilderness and Maze

The Wilderness, in the springtime a wild sea of daffodils and flowering bulbs, was originally a very formal garden, where courtiers could wander (from the German, *wilder*) through a variety of elaborate compartmentalised gardens. The most famous and popular of these was, and is still, the Maze.

11. Tennis Court

Real tennis is still played by amateurs and professionals in these galleried Stuart courts, built on the site where Henry VIII too enjoyed the 'king of games'.

12. 20th Century Garden

This lovely quiet backwater at the end of the canal was formerly a training garden for apprentice gardeners. Today you may still watch a gardener at work, one of the 39 who today look after the 24 hectares of formal gardens at Hampton Court Palace.

13. Long Water

The Long Water with its avenue of scented lime trees was created for Charles II in 1660. Four times each hour, a 15m jet of water soars into the air at the canal's furthest end. This is the Jubilee Fountain installed in 2002 to commemorate the 50th anniversary of Queen Elizabeth II's accession.

14. Chapel Court

Chapel Court houses a garden similar to one Henry VIII created at Hampton Court in the 1530s. Enclosed by low rails in the Tudor colours of green and white, it is planted with favourites of the period including primroses, violets and strawberries, and adorned with heraldic beasts, which carry the badges of Henry VIII and his succession of wives.

15. The Royal Kitchen Garden

Restored in 2014, this recreates a garden from the 18th century and is planted with rare varieties of fruit and vegetables.

16. The Magic Garden

Opened in 2016; a children's play area full of secrets and surprises!

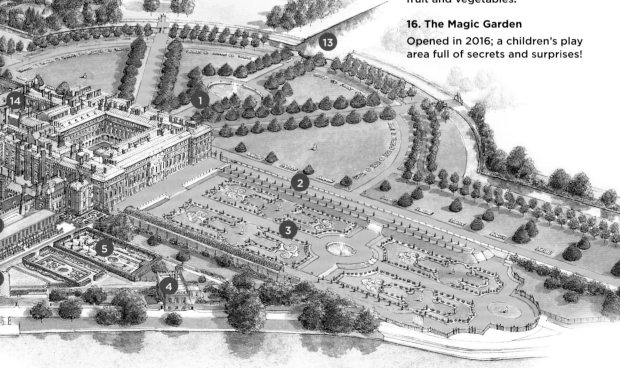

A grace-and-favour life

Following King George III's decision not to stay in Hampton Court, the palace was subdivided into accommodation of varying sizes. These grace-and-favour homes were given by the monarch in recognition of great service to crown or country. Apartments were usually awarded to single, widowed and married women, and occasionally men. The last grace-and-favour warrants were granted during the 1980s, but many traces of this fascinating era can still be seen around the palace today.

NO THOROUGHFA
PRIVATE
RESIDENTS

'We must not run down Lady Fisher on our tricycles.'

The elderly grace-and-favour residents of Hampton Court had more to fear than the odd ghost in the cloisters; visiting grandchildren posed a real danger! Here, Rachel Hall and her father, writer and broadcaster Ludovic Kennedy, recall some happy times when the palace was 'all theirs'.

My grandmother, Rosalind Kennedy, was offered a grace-and-favour apartment at Hampton Court in 1942 after the loss at sea of my grandfather, Edward Kennedy (Captain of HMS Rawalpindi which was sunk by two German battle-cruisers in November 1939). She moved to a house on the corner of Tennis Court Lane in 1943, where she lived until 1975. My aunt remembers those war years, of hearing the doodlebugs and sleeping under a table during bombing raids but also the beauty of the palace during the blackout when the cloisters were lit by flaming torches.

My grandmother's house was large, with a lovely first floor drawing room which looked west, down to the main gate and the river beyond; there were four floors and over 30 rooms which I understand were all furnished and used regularly until the mid 1960s when my grandmother felt unable to run a house of such a size. As all the grace-and-favour apartments were given for life there was no possibility of her moving to smaller apartments so the top two floors were emptied and sealed and for the next ten years my grandmother used only the ground and first floor rooms.

The kitchen was spacious, high ceilinged and resembled that of a country farmhouse; with an Esse range cooker on one side, a pulley for drying clothes above it and a scrubbed wooden table in the middle of the room. Wolsey, my grandmother's round tabby had an unusual cat flap; an entire pane of a large sash window hinged open and he would come and go as he pleased. Beyond the kitchen was a flat where the couple who helped my grandmother lived and on the other side of the kitchen was the pantry and dumb waiter, which was the food lift to the upper floors.

There was a large room on the first floor that had windows down both sides, with deep window seats and a fireplace at one end. Although this room was a thoroughfare – to reach other rooms – my grandmother nevertheless used it as her bedroom. I remember it fondly as one of the best rooms in the house, with comfy chairs near the fire and a large table in the middle of the room for games and puzzles, and sometimes my grandmother sitting up in bed the other end surrounded by newspapers.

Visiting my grandmother as a small child was a thrilling experience; we had the run of the palace and would race through the cloisters ducking under the 'No Thoroughfare' signs and out into the gardens. My cousin Roderick remembers, aged 6 or 7, going out to play with my sister Ailsa and being asked by my grandmother, 'Now what must you NOT do?'. They replied in unison, 'We must not run down Lady Fisher on our tricycles'. The cloisters were ideal for tricycling and the ramps down to the chapel

From far left to right:

Rachel's grandparents on board HMS Constance off Bermuda in 1920;

Crowds gather in Clock Court to catch a glimpse of the ballerina Moira Shearer arriving for her wedding to Ludovic Kennedy in 1950;

Ludovic and his sister Katherine before her wedding in the Chapel Royal, 1947;

Rachel, big sister Ailsa and their mother enjoying a sunny day in the orchard at the palace in 1957;

Ludovic, Moira and Rosalind Kennedy at the Palace in 1950.

door and then back up again was a great racing stretch, elderly residents stood no chance as we came round blind corners on two wheels.

My sister Ailsa recalls being on her best behaviour when taken to have tea with Lady Baden Powell.

We felt very privileged to be able to roam the palace as we wished and we knew many passages, cloisters and courts that the public never saw. Certainly the palace had quite a different mood once the public had all gone home and it was indeed wonderful to walk through the last archway from the dark echoing cloisters into the golden light that bathed the gardens and Long Water on summer evenings. My father recalls my grandmother's joy, when giving evening parties after the war, of taking her guests into the gardens and having it all to themselves.

As a resident my grandmother was able to use the palace for parties and formal occasions. Both my father and his two sisters were married in the Chapel Royal, my sister (and possibly other grandchildren) were christened there and over the years various family parties were held in the Oak Room.

Although there were many residents at the palace, the grace-and-favour apartments were so widely distributed within it that we children only knew

those well who lived in the courts nearest to my grandmother. There was Lady Birdwood whom my father remembers was an early friend, and my sister Ailsa recalls being on her best behaviour when taken to have tea with Lady Baden Powell (founder of the Girl Guides movement). My particular friend was Lady Webb Bowen whose little dachshund Monty I often walked. My grandmother's cousin Aunt Margaret (Lady Grant) lived in a nearby court; I remember her house was decorated entirely in pink and purple which, as a young girl, I naturally thought was exactly how all houses should be decorated.

There are so many memories we grandchildren share of those happy times with our generous and eccentric grandmother: the strike of the great clock at night as we lay in our beds, dressing up in splendid Edwardian clothes from her large dressing up box, scaring ourselves thoroughly in the cloisters at night, picnic tea in the old orchard, getting lost in the Maze, feeding the ducks on the Long Water, the array of baskets and ropes hanging from the apartments on the upper floors of the William and Mary 'extension', watching a game of real tennis through the netting and walking among the deer in Bushy Park on a frosty winter's day.

A palace that has been around for over 500 years has amassed a lot of statistics, some, perhaps, more vital than others!

Palace particulars

You may have counted 241 decorated chimneys yourself but did you know that it takes 33 hours per year to peel off the 2kg of chewing gum from the floors of the state apartments? (Yes, we know it's not *you* that dropped it...)

👑 How many conservators does it take to change a light bulb? Three – and one electrician! (Well, some ceilings are over 10m high, so we need to build a scaffold to get up there!)

👑 Tudor officers, yeomen and grooms at court ate over a kilo of meat every day, part of the daily personal total of around 5,000 calories. In our Tiltyard Café today, top seller is the fruit scone, with over 91,000 a year sold. (Approximately 225 calories each, however!)

👑 Over 5,000 objects are displayed, including 44 tapestries and 26 grand-scale wall paintings, tended by a team of 33 specialist conservators.

👑 Ugh! The preventive conservation team identify and record on average 8,000 insects a year. We monitor all insect activity, but make detailed records of any that are considered to be pests.

👑 Wake up! Hampton Court Palace has the largest collection of royal and state beds (five) in the country.

👑 Over 200,000 flowering bulbs are planted each year in the formal gardens and 140,000 plants grown in the nurseries.

👑 About 330,000 people go into the Maze each year ... and as far as we know, they all come out again, eventually!

👑 The oldest tree at Hampton Court is the medieval oak in Home Park, believed to be over 1,000 years old. The youngest member of staff, an admissions assistant, is 18, as we write.

Laid flat, all the tapestries at Hampton Court Palace would cover an area of six tennis courts. The 'real' tennis court here, believed to be the oldest one of its kind still in use, covers an area of 412 sq metres, which is less than half the size of the grass area of the modern Wimbledon Centre Court.

The Great Vine is 240 years old and over 36.5m long. It takes the Vine Keeper about three weeks to harvest all the sweet black dessert grapes in the autumn.

Each year, nearly 450,000 people visit the palace – and it's lovely to see you all! Just watch where you stick your chewing gum....

Above: Each of the 3,000 objects which make up the collection of arms and armour in the King's Guard Chamber is being hand-cleaned and lacquered in a specially designed studio within the palace.

Left: Tapestries are washed by hand in an adapted 24m greenhouse. Wet cleaning reduces acidity levels which helps slow down the process of degradation.

The caring profession

You may not be a fan of housework, but can you imagine polishing 4,000 silver teaspoons, or having to build a scaffold to clean your ceiling?

Looking after a historic royal palace demands housekeeping on a grand scale, but it's all in a day's work for the Conservation and Collection Care (CCC) team based at Hampton Court Palace.

The team are a group of 33 highly-trained preventive and treatment conservators and conservation scientists, who together have over 250 years of experience. They care for an amazing, diverse and often priceless collection of treasures.

As conservators, they face the daily challenge of protecting these objects from a number of hazards, including light, heat, insects and dust (mainly from visitors!) as well as planning long-term housekeeping and conservation projects. For example, the cleaning of the arms and armour collection displayed in the King's Guard Chamber (over 3,000 individual objects), took over five years to complete.

Conservators are also responsible for advising and training other palace staff, such as those who organise the increasingly popular functions and special events at the palace, including wedding receptions and parties. These events can give us an important boost to our income, enabling us to care for the palaces more effectively, but conditions have to be carefully controlled to avoid any accidental damage to our historic interiors.

Monitoring the condition of objects in our care often leads to us making discoveries that improve conservation techniques. We have been using laser-scanning techniques to measure the deterioration of the terracotta roundels and we have developed a technique to safely project coloured light onto one of Henry VIII's tapestries to show how its original colours would have dazzled visitors to the Great Hall 500 years ago. To see a video of this, and to learn more about tapestry conservation, visit 'Henry's Tapestries Revealed' on our website.

Want to know more? Just 'Ask'

We also strive to inform visitors about the work we do, explaining the techniques and skills that go into conserving the collections. Our 'Ask the Conservators' programme gives visitors a close-up glimpse of some of the work we do that normally occurs behind the scenes. Wherever possible, our major conservation projects now take place in open view, instead of hidden away in workshops. One of our most popular recent projects at Hampton Court was the conservation of the beautiful dome of Queen Charlotte's royal state bed. The bed is too fragile to move any distance, so work was carried out in Mary II's Apartments, and illustrated by regular talks from the conservators together with question and answer sessions.

When you are next at the palace, look out for our conservators, who can be identified by their 'Ask the Conservators' badges. They will be particularly interested in telling you about what they are doing to conserve the palace's collections, and are happy to answer any questions you may have.

To find out more about how you can support the essential work of caring for the collections, please visit **www.hrp.org.uk**

Conservators re-attaching the fragile embroidered silk lining to the inside of the domed roof of Queen Charlotte's 18th-century bed.

Presentations at 'Ask' events give visitors an opportunity to observe conservation in progress.

Tapestry Studio

Textile workrooms have existed at Hampton Court Palace since the beginning of the 20th century, when King Edward VII invited William Morris & Co to set up a tapestry restoration workshop. The late 19th-century policy of restoring tapestries, even reweaving whole sections, has been superseded. Conservation now supports, strengthens and preserves the original material.

Four more palaces to explore;
hundreds of stories to discover

Tower of London

Gaze up at the massive White Tower, tiptoe through a king's medieval bedchamber and marvel at the Crown Jewels. Meet the Yeoman Warders with bloody tales to tell; stand where famous heads rolled and prisoners wept ... then discover even more surprising stories about the Tower!

Banqueting House

Walk in the footsteps of a dazzling company of courtiers who once danced, drank and partied beneath Rubens's magnificent painted ceiling. This revolutionary building was created for court entertainments, but is probably most famous for the execution of Charles I in 1649. Spare him a thought as you gaze up at this ravishing painting – one of his last sights on earth...

Kew Palace and Queen Charlotte's Cottage

Step into this tiny doll's house of a palace and experience the joys and sorrows of King George III and his family through a radio play and displays of fascinating personal artefacts. Stroll to Queen Charlotte's Cottage, built in 1770, where the royal family enjoyed picnics and peace in a tranquil corner of Kew Gardens.

Open April to October. Admission to Kew Palace and Queen Charlotte's Cottage is included in the entry to Kew Gardens.

Kensington Palace

Take the journey of a courtier through the splendid King's Apartments and marvel at the exquisite 18th-century court dress. Discover the private and personal secrets revealed within the Queen's Apartments or explore the life of Queen Victoria in the rooms where she grew up, before enjoying a delicious cream tea in the elegant Orangery.

We offer an exciting programme of events and exhibitions throughout the year. For more information and details on tickets and how to find us, please visit www.hrp.org.uk

Supporting us

Historic Royal Palaces is the independent charity that looks after the Tower of London, Hampton Court Palace, the Banqueting House, Kensington Palace and Kew Palace. Our aim is to help everyone explore the story of how monarchs and people have shaped society in some of the greatest palaces ever built.

We receive no funding from the Government or the Crown so we depend on the support of our visitors, members, donors, volunteers and sponsors.

Can you help?

We hope you thoroughly enjoyed your visit to Hampton Court Palace and have discovered more about the conservation of this magnificent building. Our work goes on; funds will always be needed to protect and maintain Hampton Court. Your donation means this valuable work can continue.

Please call our Development Department on **020 3166 6321** for more information or email **development@hrp.org.uk**

Join us!

Joining Historic Royal Palaces is the perfect way to explore the stories inside five extraordinary places that helped define this nation's history. What's more, you'll save money and contribute to the important work of conserving the palaces at the same time.

Membership is amazing value; it gives you the freedom to visit the Tower of London, Hampton Court Palace, the Banqueting House, Kensington Palace and Kew Palace (from April to October) as often as you like.

It also means you don't have to queue – simply walk in to experience and understand what makes the palaces extraordinary. Other benefits include exclusive members-only events, behind-the-scenes tours and great discounts in our shops and online.

Make a present of the past

As you step through the doors of a royal palace you enter the realm of strategy, intrigue, ambition, romance, devotion and disaster. What more inspiring gift could there be than a Historic Royal Palaces membership for someone with a love of history and amazing buildings with their beautiful contents and gorgeous gardens?

Enquire about becoming a member of Historic Royal Palaces and find out more about the range of benefits by calling **0844 482 7788** or visiting us online at **www.hrp.org.uk/supportus**

Further reading

Grace & Favour: The Hampton Court Palace Community 1750-1950
Sarah E Parker, Historic Royal Palaces, 2005

Hampton Court: A Social and Architectural History
Simon Thurley, Yale University Press, 2003

The Story of Hampton Court Palace
Lucy Worsley and David Souden
Merrell in association with Historic Royal Palaces, 2015

The Story of the Gardens at Hampton Court Palace
Historic Royal Palaces, 2016

Henry VIII: 500 Facts
Brett Dolman et al, Historic Royal Palaces, 2009

A Really Useful Guide to the Tudors
Sarah Kilby and David Souden, Historic Royal Palaces, 2015

The Taste of the Fire: The Story of the Tudor Kitchens at Hampton Court Palace, Historic Royal Palaces, 2007

For children
Henry's Blog
Elizabeth Newbery, Historic Royal Palaces, 2009

Power Palace: Tales from Hampton Court
Elizabeth Newbery, Historic Royal Palaces, 2006

Historic Royal Palaces

Historic Royal Palaces is the charity that looks after:

Tower of London
Hampton Court Palace
Banqueting House
Kensington Palace
Kew Palace
Hillsborough Castle

We help everyone explore the story of how monarchs and people have shaped society, in some of the greatest palaces ever built.

We raise all our own funds and depend on the support of our visitors, members, donors, sponsors and volunteers.

ACCREDITED
MUSEUM

Acknowledgements

The following institutions and individuals have made loans of works of art or contributions to Hampton Court Palace. Their help is gratefully acknowledged here:

(Funding and supporting bodies) The Art Fund, The Department for Culture, Media and Sport and Arts Council England.

(Lenders) The Trustees of the 9th Duke of Buccleuch's Chattels Fund. The National Portrait Gallery, London. The Government Art Collection of the United Kingdom. The Trustees of the British Museum. The Ashmolean Museum, Oxford. The Victoria & Albert Museum, London. The Board of Trustees of National Museums Liverpool (Lady Lever Art Gallery). Hereford Museum and Art Gallery. The Trustees of the 5th Marquis Camden. The Trustees of the NR Coville Will Trust. The Trustees of the Ilchester Family Arrangement Trust. The Trustees of the A H Whiteley Settlement and various other private individuals.

Published by Historic Royal Palaces
Hampton Court Palace
Surrey
KT8 9AU

© Historic Royal Palaces 2016

All rights reserved. No part of this publication may be reproduced or transmitted in any form or by any means electronic or mechanical, including photocopying, recording or any information storage and retrieval system, without permission in writing from the publisher.

ISBN 978-1-873993-06-4

Written by Brett Dolman (tour 1), Sebastian Edwards (history, tours 3, 4 and 5), Susanne Groom (tour 6) and Marc Meltonville (tour 2).

With acknowledgements to Tom Campbell for his research and advice on Henry VIII's tapestry collection.

Edited by Sarah Kilby and Clare Murphy
Picture sourcing: Annie Heron and Susan Mennell
Designed by www.brandremedy.com
Principal photography by Robin Forster and Nick Guttridge
Illustration inside front cover and pages 64-65 by Stephen Conlin
Cartoon illustrations by Tim Archbold: 13, 34bl, 70-71

Printed by CPI Colour

Illustrations
Unless otherwise stated all illustrations are Crown Copyright: Historic Royal Palaces or © Historic Royal Palaces.

Abbreviations: b = bottom; c = centre; l = left; r = right; t = top

Baron (private collection): 68tc, 69tr; The British Library: 9br; The Trustees of the British Museum: 6-7, 8tl; The College of Arms, London: 8b; Rachel Hall (private collection) 68tl, 68tr, 69tl; © Historic Royal Palaces/newsteam.co.uk: 4c, 16, 27br, 30-31, 32b, 33tr, 44-45; Kunsthistorisches Museum, Vienna: 12(inset: 3); The London Fire Brigade 11br; The Louvre Museum, Paris: 12 (inset: 4); National Gallery of Art, Washington, DC/The Bridgeman Art Library: 9tl; The Board of Trustees of the National Museums and Galleries on Merseyside (The Walker Art Gallery, Liverpool): 12; National Portrait Gallery, London: 12(insets: 1,2,6), 37br, 57t; The Royal Collection © 2013 HM Queen Elizabeth II: 12(inset: 5), 15(inset), 17, 22, 23, 24-25, 36, 37bl, 40tl, 40tr, 49tr, 51, 52t, 52b, 54-55, 56, 57t, 57b, 59; David Utting: 43br; V & A Images/Victoria and Albert Museum: 25b; Warburg Institute: 32tl

Historic Royal Palaces is a registered charity
(no 1068852)
www.hrp.org.uk

 Find us on Facebook: **Historic Royal Palaces**

Follow us on Twitter **@HRP_palaces**

 Watch us: **www.youtube.com/HistoricRoyalPalaces**